MARAUDER M

KENNETH T. BROWN served in the B-26 Marauder during World War II, then used the G.I. Bill to complete his undergraduate education at Swarthmore College in Pennsylvania and obtain a doctorate in physiological psychology at the University of Chicago. After further training under postdoctoral fellowships, he had a long career as a distinguished professor of neurophysiology at the University of California Medical School in San Francisco. In retirement he remains in San Francisco, where he designs and makes furniture for his family and friends.

AVAILABLE NOW

MARAUDER MAN

The Story of the Medium Bomber
That Made D-Day Possible

A Memoir/History

Kenneth T. Brown

ibooks
new york
www.ibooks.net

DISTRIBUTED BY SIMON & SCHUSTER

An ibooks, inc. Book

All rights reserved, including the right to reproduce this
book or portions thereof in any form whatsoever.
Distributed by Simon & Schuster, Inc.
1230 Avenue of the Americas, New York, NY 10020

ibooks, inc.
24 West 25th Street
New York, NY 10010

The ibooks World Wide Web Site address is:
http://www.ibooks.net

Copyright © 2001 by Kenneth T. Brown
Reprinted with permission of Pacifica Military History

ISBN: 0-7434-7929-7
First ibooks printing March 2004
10 9 8 7 6 5 4 3 2 1

To Chapin and Bonde,
 My frequent pilots and fellow warriors,
 Who always brought me home.

And to Ginnie,
 My wife and playmate,
 Who made it all worthwhile.

'Tis all a Chequer board of Nights and Days
Where Destiny with Men for Pieces plays:
    Hither and thither moves, and mates, and slays,
And one by one back in the Closet lays.

—Edward FitzGerald, trans.
Rubaiyat of Omar Khayyam

Contents

Foreword

Worid War II was truly a defining event, both in American history and in the lives of those who participated in widely varying roles. This applied so strongly in my case that I have often felt the urge to write of my experiences, and with time running out, the desire finally became irresistible.

My growing up as a Quaker farm boy was typical of rural America at that time. During the Great Depression and between two great wars, close behind our country's pioneer era and with the postwar high-tech era still well ahead, it was a time of slow pace and hard work. Still rightly evoking nostalgia, in retrospect it was a good time to approach adulthood and is presented here as background to all that came later in my life. I also describe how, while barely of draft age, my thinking evolved from conscientious objection to air warrior, exemplifying the difficult decisions thrust upon so many of us while still so young.

Following seventeen months of training, my experience of war included intense combat, brushes with historic events, and human interest stories of various kinds. Among my forty-three combat missions the untold story of one, which I feel uniquely qualified to chronicle, is so extraordinary and dramatic that I felt especially compelled to relate it in Chapter 17, "The Ordeal by Flak of Flight 4."

My missions were experienced from seldom-discussed and little-known crew positions. Although the role of pilots is well known, I was trained as a bombardier-navigator. In combat, I worked initially in that role, followed by a longer period as lead navigator for groups of planes including full mission formations.

Most notably, however, published accounts of aerial warfare during World War II have strongly emphasized four-engine heavy bombers, the B-17s and B-24s used in a strategic role to bomb factories and cities, plus single-engine fighters and dive-bombers. But I served in the B-26 Martin Marauder, a twin-engine medium bomber used tactically in support of troop operations. In design, it was the most advanced medium bomber of its time. However, in spite of its outstanding performance, extensive use, and the critical importance of its operations, this plane has remained little known. Thus the contributions of the thousands of people who designed, built, flew, and maintained this remarkable aircraft have never been appropriately recognized. In response to this need, I also include here factual information about the B-26 itself, how its operations were conducted, and its historic role in World War II, based upon written materials and interviews in addition to my own experience. The facts thus acquired should speak for themselves, and though given with unabashed admiration for both the plane and the men I knew who flew it, there is no conscious embellishment. Indeed, in view of the need for an accurate perspective, I have come to think of this book as my final mission with the B-26.

One may wonder, with good reason, about the validity of memories from so long ago. But wartime combat is so charged with emotion that certain images and events are retained with almost crystalline clarity. Also, many memories have been reinforced while being related to family or friends, and even now they sometimes run through my mind unbidden. Whenever uncertain of a point and it was possible to do so, I checked details with old friends and acquaintances from the war, archival consultants, or written materials. Although I didn't keep a diary, I kept a record of my combat missions and wrote to my parents almost every other day while overseas. I kept those letters after my parents died and recently read them in chronological sequence. They could not contain anything about our operations, but they were helpful regarding other aspects of my life during the war. Despite these precautions, some details may have become blurred in memory without adequate backup from other sources, and any such errors are entirely my own.

Chapter 1

Family and Farm Beginnings

W hen Pearl Harbor propelled our country into war, I was nineteen years of age, having been raised in northern Virginia near the small town of Purcellville, about fifty miles west of Washington, D.C. This was Loudoun County, neither North nor South, but country that had been raged over many times by both armies during the Civil War. From that time, I still have the musket of my maternal grandfather, David H. Birdsall. Although he was not a combatant, he was once fired upon as a suspected spy while carrying his musket home from squirrel hunting. I was raised in the home, and on part of the dairy farm, that he established. My mother, Gertrude, inherited this property and continued to use it as a farm until her death.

My mother and father were second cousins, and my father's parents were also raised near Purcellville. However, in 1884, as part of the great western movement of that time, my paternal grandfather migrated with his wife and infant first son to Nebraska. He homesteaded near Genoa, which is still only a small town, and my father, Ralph, was born there in 1886. The family eventually had nine children, of whom only one died in infancy, an unusually low infant mortality for that time. Living in a sod house, the only kind that could be built in that vast prairie where there was almost no wood, they homesteaded successfully and "proved up" the land so that they owned it. But it was a terribly hard life, especially the winters. So, after about twelve years there, when my father was ten years of age, my grandfather joined two other families in an idealistic kind of commune that migrated to Georgia. Arriving before winter, they planned to have survival crops planted and harvested for winter food. However, the plantation where they settled had been devoted solely to cotton for so long that nothing edible could be grown from the soil, and they literally faced starvation. The children foraged in the fields and woods, and often the only thing they could find was wild onions. So my father retained bitter memories of those times and could never again bring himself to eat onions.

Their plantation was near a river that flowed south into the Gulf of Mexico, near Apalachicola in the Florida panhandle, and Grandfather had heard seafood was plentiful there on the Gulf Coast. So they built a large raft for the family and all their possessions, including a wagon and horses. The labor required can only be imagined, and with so little food it must have been a terrible task. But they completed it, then loaded up everything and floated down to the coast, where Grandfather became one of the first settlers on the mainland side of Apalachicola Bay. Seafood indeed proved plentiful, and many years later, when I visited as a child, one could still gather as many wild oysters as desired by just walking along the beaches. Now Apalachicola oysters have become famous.

The sea also provided building material for their home. A schooner had come into the bay to take shelter from a storm, and it was carrying lumber on its decks. The storm proved fierce, and the deck lumber probably made the schooner top-heavy. In any case, it foundered, and the deck lumber broke loose and floated ashore, where it was salvaged by my grandfather's family and used to build a substantial house. When I last visited the area, this house was still intact, and by now it has probably become a historic landmark in the town of Eastpoint, which has grown around it.

Prior to building the house, Grandfather had somehow acquired enough land for a farm, where he raised sugarcane and converted it into molasses. Before me, as I write, is a memento of the family's early days in Eastpoint, a framed sample of the classy labels for their cans of molasses. It says:

Bay Croft Brand
Pure Cane
SYRUP
Manufactured by
D. H. Brown, Eastpoint, Fla.

During my childhood we visited Grandfather's home in Florida, from which I have an especially fond memory. Eastpoint was still a small fishing village with no post office. So Grandfather, in addition to all his other work, served as postmaster. This was done from a large, old-fashioned desk in his living room, and the mail was sorted into pigeonholes, one for each family in Eastpoint. The house was never locked, and at any time of the day or night one of the local residents might amble in to collect the mail from his family's pigeonhole. If any of Grandfather's family were in the living room, the local resident might sit down and chat for a while, then get up and leave as casually as he had entered. It was as if the entire village were part of an extended family centered around Grandfather's home. Indeed, in many ways that was the case. No one in the family seemed to mind the loss of privacy, which was more than repaid by the warm feeling of being part of such a closely knit community.

This story of my father's family is a vivid reminder of how closely my generation followed the pioneer era of our country. My father bridged the gap, spending his childhood as one of the early settlers and then living to see things he could never have imagined from that sod house on the Nebraska prairie.

When my mother was a young woman, she and a girlfriend went to Florida to visit the part of her family that had migrated there by way of Nebraska and Georgia. At that time, marriages between second cousins were rather common, and she was courted by both Uncle Herbert and my father, who won the day. He was then about twenty-seven years of age and was still going barefoot much of the time, having worked since a small boy on his father's farms. His education was minimal and probably typical for farm children of those times. He had completed grammar school, then managed to do two years of high school in the same year, before quitting to work full-time on the farm. However, he had dreamed of other things, and falling in love with my mother was the turning point. So about a year after her visit he traveled to Washington, D.C., where he arrived with only ten dollars in his pocket. After working as a streetcar conductor for another year, he married my mother and moved to her farm.

Soon thereafter he started working in Purcellville, only a mile away, where he was employed by the Loudoun Light and Power Company, one of many small, independent power companies that dotted the country in those days. Many power companies of that time made ice, which was delivered by truck to iceboxes in the homes of their customers, home refrigerators having not yet become available. This provided my father's first job, working in the ice plant ten hours every day except Sunday, at the company's minimum salary of twelve dollars a week. But he took a correspondence course in electrical engineering and thereafter advanced rapidly to become manager of the company. He also continued working on our farm. Most notably, he rose with my mother at 4:00 A.M. to help milk the cows and do the morning chores before breakfast. This was true even on weekdays, when he thereafter spent a full workday at his regular job. Also, during evenings and weekends he often worked in our large garden, where we grew almost all of our own produce.

Mother always kept several cows and, until her death at seventy-three, did most of the farmwork. This included caring for and milking the cows, straining and storing the milk, then selling it to customers who came to our home. We were on the main road west from Washington, and people on outings from the capital often stopped at our "Milk for Sale" sign. At harvesttime, Mother also worked in the fields, being as capable there as any other farmworker. Of course, she also did most of the housework. Typical of farm families in those times, she prepared three large meals a day, each including meat and a variety of other dishes. She was justifiably proud of her cooking and expected anyone at her table to eat a portion from every dish. This was difficult to avoid because she somehow kept track of what each of us had eaten, and at the end of the meal she would pointedly offer anything that had been missed. So we ate very well, probably too well, but this was long before cholesterol became a household word. Fortunately, in those times even families of modest means could afford domestic help. In our case, we had a long-standing arrangement with two middle-aged sisters who came to our house one day each week. While one cleaned the house, the other baked for the coming week, which relieved Mother from enough housework to make her other work possible.

Mother's cows were critical to the family finances during the early years of her marriage, and though they later became unnecessary from that point of view, she loved them and could never bring herself to give them up. Unfortunately, they had to be milked at 4:00 A.M. and 4:00 P.M. every day, without exception; otherwise they would have "dried up." So our lives were severely confined by this schedule. On weekends the only family getaways we could manage were short drives to nearby places, but even these were fraught with anxiety because flat tires and unexpected delays were common, and a delayed return meant cows bawling in pain at the barnyard gate. True vacations were even more difficult to arrange because they required someone else to take care of the cows. I only recall two of these, both to visit my father's relatives in Florida. Under those conditions I couldn't share my mother's fondness for cows and, indeed, came to think of them as large lead weights about the family neck.

I had no brothers but a sister, who was several years older. Ruth helped Mother in the kitchen, and we learned as children how to milk cows, each being assigned one of the easier cows during the evening milking. I also learned many other chores and did farmwork of increasing difficulty and amount as I grew older and stronger. Our heavy farmwork in those days was still done with horses, so we had all the horse-drawn devices needed for our type of farming, including plows, harrows, a sledge for clearing rocks from the land, a mowing machine and hay rake, a large hay wagon, and a light "spring wagon" for hauling loads to and from town. We no longer kept horses ourselves, but my mother's only sister, Aunt Lillian, lived just down the road and had a team we sometimes borrowed. Also, in those days some farm laborers kept a team of horses and hired themselves and the horses out by the day. I was only seven in 1929, so almost all the childhood I remember was during the Great Depression, when a man and his team could be hired for two dollars a day.

We had only a few cows and about forty acres of land—some in pasture, some in hay, and the rest in cash crops such as corn and wheat. The heaviest work, such as plowing, was hired out. But we did much of the rest ourselves. For example, our hay wagon was often pulled by Aunt Lillian's pair of horses at haymaking time. Mother and I used pitchforks to throw up the heavy, only partially dried hay, while a hired hand distributed the hay on the wagon and controlled the horses. The work became harder as the wagon was piled higher, until the pitchfork at full reach barely put the hay onto the wagon. I well remember this because haymaking was done in the hottest part of late summer, and no straw hat of any size could keep the chaff from filtering down inside our shirt collars. When the wagon was fully loaded it was driven into the upper level of our barn (the haymow), where we unloaded it.

At age fourteen, I received for Christmas the heart's desire of every country boy I knew. This one was a .22-caliber, bolt-action, single-shot Winchester. In those days, farmboys frequently hunted small game to supplement the family meat supply, and I had longed to do this. So I became a squirrel hunter, literally following my grandfather's footsteps into the woods behind our farm. It was small but big enough for me, and I quickly came to love it, both the woods itself and the challenge of learning to hunt squirrels. One of Mother's Washington milk customers was a man who especially liked squirrel meat, so he would stop by in the morning to let me know he was in the area. He then continued his excursion while I went squirrel hunting, and on his way home he stopped to pick up what I had bagged. After dressing them out myself he paid me twenty-five cents each, and on one notable occasion I got three. This was good money in those days, especially for a boy of my age, because carpenters and farm laborers were only getting about twenty cents an hour. So this became my first experience of making good money while doing something I enjoyed. I later realized that this is a sound and useful principle; the more one enjoys his work, the better he will be at it, and the more financially rewarding it probably will become.

At that time, Sears, Roebuck sold trapping supplies by mail and also bought the dried skins of skunks and opossums, both of which were plentiful in the woods where I hunted. So one winter I also set out a trapline, which was dutifully run every day, on one occasion even during a blizzard. Skinning the opossums was all right, but I should have sought instruction before trying that first skunk. Also, a little later a trapped skunk got me on the foot before I dispatched it. By the time I reached home, I could no longer smell the odor myself, but Mother smelled me from our house while I was returning through the barnyard. After I took a bath and changed clothes, my shoes were still suspect, but by then Mother couldn't smell the odor either. Since I had only one pair of shoes, she took the precaution of putting some perfume on them and sent me off to school. Upon arriving I was told that I smelled like two different things, skunk and perfume. Instead of the one disguising the other, the mixture was horrible. So I was banished to the very back of the schoolroom for the entire day, and it took a long time to outlive the nickname "Polecat Brown." This brought my trapping career to an abrupt end and taught me another useful lesson. You can't win them all!

In my later teens I helped Aunt Lillian's son Howell, who was fourteen years older than I, with projects on their poultry farm. One summer we dug out a full basement, under one of their poultry houses, to provide space for large incubators in which chicks were hatched out from eggs. I did most of the digging by hand, while Howell worked the horses, using a heavy scoop to move the earth out and dump it. Later, using similar methods, we dug out and dammed a pool large enough for swimming in the creek that ran through their property. The pool wasn't very big, but I learned to swim there—sort of. Not long afterward a heavy storm washed away the dam, and we didn't have the heart to rebuild it.

In the summer when I was seventeen, Howell and I tore down a barn and built a large two-story chicken house. The foundation was a concrete slab 22 by 44 feet and 4 inches thick, all of which I mixed. We had a small gasoline-powered mixer, but for each load I had to shovel the cement and gravel into the mixer, add the necessary water, and after mixing, lower the concrete into a wheelbarrow. Howell then trundled the wheelbarrow to where the concrete was needed, dumped it, and smoothed it into the growing floor. This process seemed to go on forever, and now I know why. That floor required about 323 cubic feet of concrete, and each mix was only about 1 cubic foot, so it was a huge job. No wonder it seemed we would never get that building off the ground. The carpentry was easy by comparison, though there was a great deal of it. But then, for the roof, we applied three coats of hot tar and tarpaper during the hottest part of the summer. The sun was beating down from above, while the black tar and tarpaper were radiating heat from below like a furnace, and we were in between. Add the messiness of working with hot liquid tar, and this was probably the most unpleasant work I ever did. However, I was being paid, and my wages were appropriate for those late-Depression days in 1939, two dollars for a ten-hour day, which I worked six days a week. These were the same wages and hours of my father's job in the ice plant more than twenty years before.

My mother and father were both Quakers, adhering to the original form of that faith, which emphasizes that each person has equal access to God, with no need of intermediary priests or ministers. On my father's side, the original Quaker ancestors of his father and mother came to this country in 1677 and 1683, respectively. My mother's ancestors are less known to me, but they probably arrived in America at about the same time, during the early settlement of Pennsylvania under the influence of William Penn. In any event, through my father I am among the ninth generation of Quakers in this country. I cannot take pride in this, since it is not of my making, but I am pleased it is so. As a result, I was raised in the Quaker faith in the Goose Creek Monthly Meeting of Friends in Lincoln, Virginia, a small village about two miles from Purcellville that remains almost unchanged from the time of my childhood.

I have described this childhood background because it strongly shaped my life in ways for which I am grateful. In particular, I learned hard work of many kinds and an abiding respect for fundamental values. Also, with very busy parents, an older sister with whom I had little in common, and no brothers or nearby neighbor children, I grew up lonely. This was a great hardship at the time, but it became a blessing because it taught me to appreciate solitude and the companionship of my own thoughts, which encouraged independence of thought and spirit. These influences served me well during World War II, as in all other aspects of my life.

The public schools in our area and time provided the fundamentals of education but otherwise left much to be desired. The consolidated high school was in Lincoln and drew children together by bus from a radius of almost ten miles. Even so, the graduating class each year was only about fifty students, most of whom would continue their family traditions of farming. There was little attention to preparation for college, and only one or two students from each graduating class went to college. In this situation my parents wisely sent me, for the last two years of high school, to a college preparatory (prep) school.

The one they chose was George School, a coeducational boarding school founded by Quakers and located at Newtown, near Philadelphia.

Ruth had preceded me there and remembers taking an English course from James Michener, who later served in the navy during World War II and soon thereafter became famous for his *Tales of the South Pacific*. Although none of my own teachers became so renowned, I probably learned more there in a week than I had ever learned previously in months of schooling. In fact, the academic preparation was so thorough that much I encountered in the first year of college had already been covered at George School.

I was also greatly helped there in ways unrelated to the curriculum. My daily life was no longer governed by the milking schedule of cows, and the newfound freedom was wonderful. Even more important, I was freed from the bullying to which I had been subjected in our rural public schools. Bullying came naturally to some of the farmboys, and I was an easy target. I didn't like to fight, and always lost when I tried, because my heart wasn't in it and I didn't know how. In retrospect, this probably wouldn't have happened if I had grown up with brothers, because the friendly wrestling of boys teaches them how to wrestle. In any event, bullying had made me excessively timid and greatly lacking in confidence.

At George School the problem disappeared because bullying was almost unknown there, nor would it have been tolerated by our mentors. Also, sports were required, and in the winter I took up wrestling, for which we had an excellent coach. After my first year I was one of the best in my weight class, but I couldn't make the varsity in my second and last year because Gus Cadwallader was an outstanding wrestler. I made the junior varsity, however, by beating Bill Marble in a match I will never forget. We were so even in technique, speed, strength, and endurance that by the end of regulation time in the match we were almost exhausted. Neither of us had achieved an advantage in points, so it went into a 2½-minute period of overtime and then into another such period. Finally, with about thirty seconds to go in the second overtime, I pinned him and won the match. Being too exhausted to stand, I crawled to the sidelines and didn't move again for about half an hour. But I couldn't have been happier, having proved myself in a way I hadn't realized was possible. This did wonders for my self-esteem and became a breakthrough in becoming immunized to bullying, whether physical or otherwise. By this time

I had also learned what a mistake it is to give in to bullying, since the most effective way to neutralize a bully of any kind is to beat him thoroughly, and as soon as possible, at his own game.

Indeed, George School was one of the most important turning points of my life. It not only increased my self-awareness and confidence, it also opened many doors to the wider world that I had hardly even dreamed of, let alone experienced. This included especially the fellowship of lively minds, scholarship, and the love of learning; as well as the friendship of people my own age of both sexes, something I had never known before.

At this Quaker school I likewise learned more about that faith. Most pertinent to this account is the Quaker testimony against war. Because of this, many Quakers register in wartime as conscientious objectors, who testify that for religious reasons they cannot conscientiously take a human life, even during war. I gave much thought to this and was so convinced it would be my course in wartime that my senior essay was titled "I Object."

Chapter 2
From Conscientous Objector to B-26s

O nly a year and a half later, while attending Miami University in Oxford, Ohio, I was forced by the Japanese attack on Pearl Harbor to make a final decision on this matter. The wartime draft was already in place, and I would soon have to register as a conscientious objector or become available for conscription into the armed forces. It was a very difficult decision. Finally, I took a long walk to clarify my thoughts. I was against taking human life, even in wartime, if this could be avoided. But I had to decide whether I could not purposely kill, even under the circumstances that prevailed during World War II. When pushed to the wall on this point, I finally realized that I could kill in good conscience under those conditions.

Several thoughts were critical to this decision. Many innocent lives were already being taken by ruthless regimes in Germany and Japan, and this would obviously continue indefinitely if not stopped. So the issue was not *whether* people would be killed during the war, but *who* would be killed, the aggressors or their helpless victims. It was also clear that winning World War II was essential if life in the United States, or anywhere else in the free world of that time, were to remain free. So winning that war seemed important enough to justify almost anything, even killing, especially since anyone I killed would be among those threatening us and already killing innocents in vast numbers. In short, I decided that I could not hold sacrosanct the lives of our enemies under the conditions of World War II.

I also realized that pacifism, a much broader concept than conscientious objection, is almost useless in wartime. When a country starts a war of aggression, based upon long-term planning and a massive commitment of resources, its decision is made and its leaders are deaf to righteous pleading or logical argument. Thus the most practical course is simply to win the war against the aggressor as quickly as possible. Indeed, that is often the most humane course as well, because lives may be saved on both sides by winning a war quickly and efficiently. But pacifism does have the potential to prevent or at least delay war; hence the best time to be a useful pacifist is during periods of peace.

My remaining decision was whether to wait until drafted or sign up for a reserve officer training program. The Army, Navy, and Army Air Forces (AAF) all had similar programs of that type. They required two years of college, and I had acquired the necessary second year by summer school in 1941, plus extra courses in the fall semester. We would be left in college until needed, and when called up would go into an officer training program. That sounded pretty good, so I chose the Army Air Forces and signed up. I could claim that I "volunteered," but this would only be a euphemism for avoiding the draft by doing something more palatable and more on my own terms.

As a farmboy I had already seen enough mud and muck to last a lifetime, so the ground forces were the least attractive alternative. Also, I had been raised too far from the ocean to have developed any special love for water, and could not swim well, so the Navy wasn't very appealing either. On the other hand, the Army Air Forces seemed a relatively clean and comfortable way to fight, and I was young enough to consider flying rather romantic. Such was the feeling in those days, before flying became a popular and routine way to travel.

I was called up in late February 1943, and after being inducted at Cincinnati, Ohio, traveled in civilian clothing to Keesler Field, on the Gulf Coast near Biloxi, Mississippi. The American train system was stretched to the limit by wartime troop and freight travel, so we encountered frequent delays while our train backed into sidings and waited for other trains with higher priorities. Thus the trip took three nights and two days. Also, our train was packed to full capacity, with every seat taken and no place to lie down. When cramped muscles needed stretching, this could only be done by standing up and moving around a little in the aisle. But the train was so full that even the aisles were crowded. Adding especially to our discomfort was the effect of so many bodies on the air we had to breathe. Apparently the ventilation system was inadequate, at least in our passenger car, because the air quickly became humid, starved of oxygen, and over-loaded with carbon dioxide. Also, with no one able to bathe, the air became increasingly malodorous as our trip progressed. The windows could be opened, as could the doors at the ends of the cars. However, this couldn't be tolerated for long because it was midwinter. Also, our locomotive was a coal burner, so whenever we opened a window or a door the soot filtered in, coated everything, and fouled the air in its own way. As in many other difficult situations, the best we could do was to keep changing our disadvantages. When the air became unbearably stale we opened the windows or doors, and when the cold or soot became unbearable we closed them. Proceeding in that manner, the trip seemed endless, and upon arrival we were grimy, sleep-deprived, and almost exhausted. In consequence, I remember thinking that those in charge couldn't have designed a better way to speed our transition from civilian to military life. Accustomed to being treated as individuals, with our private needs considered, by the time we arrived I already felt like only a small unit in a large body of men, unified by a common purpose that could be attained only by carrying out the orders of others, despite whatever hardships those orders entailed.

We arrived at Keesler Field shortly after dawn, and our official conversion to army privates for a month of basic training began immediately. First, sergeants assembled us into rough formations and marched us from the train to a building where we were given govern-ment issue (GI) clothes. Then we were assigned to barracks, each of which contained long lines of army cots and a facility that served all the occupants as toilet and washroom. After locating our assigned barracks, we washed up and donned our new uniforms. It then became obvious that we represented many more body types and sizes than were recognized in making GI clothing, much of which fitted poorly and hung on us in a haphazard manner. Of course, these uniforms made us all look like carbon copies, and the effect was greatly enhanced by the drabness and poor fit. So this was another big step toward losing the individuality we had enjoyed as civilians. In those days, members of the armed forces were required to wear their uniforms at all times, even when off base or on rare home leaves. So our civilian clothes were packed up and shipped home, a process that was not only practical but highly symbolic, because with them went the last visible aspects of our civilian lives.

Each of us selected a cot, with the preferred locations being close to both the toilet and a window. I was not in time for any of those, but I made a mental note to be quicker at our next posting. Regardless of location, each man's cot became his only private space at Keesler Field. Although we were called privates, it struck me as a misnomer because we had almost no privacy. Waking or sleeping, we were surrounded by many others, to whose personalities, habits, and idiosyncracies we were almost constantly subjected. For me, the most obvious and troublesome problem was at night, when a single heavy snorer could disturb the sleep of everyone in the barracks. Fortunately, we were young enough that snoring was not common, but there almost always proved to be at least one snorer, and sometimes several, in such a large barracks. So we also had to learn adaptability and forbearance toward the many other men close around us. I must confess, however, that I never became accustomed to snoring.

The main purpose of our stay at Keesler was to indoctrinate us into army life and provide a foundation for our later specialized training, so we spent much time in close-order drill and calisthenics. We were told that the drilling was to instill discipline, which it may have done. To my mind, however, it was mainly a way of moving troops around on foot in good order, with little additional value in a modern army. Indeed, the emphasis upon drilling seemed to me largely an outmoded tradition from earlier times when wars were fought almost entirely by massed foot soldiers. In any event, we did a lot of it. By contrast, the calisthenics were obviously important for physical conditioning, because aviators sometimes had to endure physical ordeals, the outcome of which determined the success or failure of a mission, or indeed the survival of the aviators. We were also given a variety of inoculations against infectious diseases. The schedule of shots was such that on one day we received three different inoculations, which we joked about as the "triple threat" because it made many of us, including myself, sick and confined to barracks for a few days. We also received our first lecture about the dangers of venereal disease, illustrated by horror pictures of what could happen to men who didn't avoid the problem altogether or take appropriate precautions. Even so, apparently the medical personnel had little confidence in the effectiveness of this type of lecture, because it was given repeatedly, with only slight variations, during our further training.

Being in the traditional Deep South for the first time, I wanted to experience the nearby area and its people. However, typical of life in the armed forces at that time, we were so focused upon training for the war that little opportunity was provided for contact with civilians in the nearby area. The only exception was a few weekend evenings, when we attended a recreational facility for servicemen that was operated by the United Service Organizations. Such facilities, known as USOs, were available in a great many American towns during World War II. The one in Biloxi provided music and dancing and was attended by many local girls. Most of these were from a small girls' college, of the type known then as a "finishing school," which taught mainly the arts, culture, and social graces deemed appropriate for a girl in southern society. So they were pleasant company and good dancers, which was all I needed or could hope for at that time.

After basic training we became aviation cadets, which was a rank of its own with special cadet uniforms, and we scattered in smaller groups to schools serving as college training detachments (CTDs). The one I attended for about six weeks was at Eastern Tennessee State Teachers College in Johnson City, Tennessee. There we took courses to assure that we had a basic knowledge of certain subjects, such as college algebra. Since most of us already had more of those subjects than provided at the CTD, it was pretty dull stuff. More valuable was the physical training in the form of calisthenics and long runs, which whipped us into still better physical condition. But the high point was the ten hours of dual instruction in a Piper Cub to learn the rudiments of flying. That was good fun and made us feel we were on our way with the kind of training we had been anticipating. In fact, none of my later time in the air matched the thrill and sheer exhilaration of flying that small plane, where the air could be felt as a living thing, substantial and supportive, and the sky was an exciting new place where I began to feel at home.

Our next posting was to Nashville, Tennessee, where we spent about two months at the AAF classification center. There we lived in tarpaper barracks during the hottest part of the summer, and many of us learned a few new things about discomfort from heat. This was made more severe by being quarantined to our own barracks areas for about the first month. I assume this was because we had come from many different places, and they wished to prevent an outbreak of disease in one barracks area from spreading to all the others. However, cadets who had completed their quarantine were allowed to wander into any of the other barracks areas, so it is hard to see how the "quarantine" could have been effective.

There was little relief from the heat, and some enterprising cadets who had completed their quarantine did a brisk business buying pints of ice cream from the post exchange (PX) for fifteen cents each and selling them in quarantined areas for twenty-five cents. This looked like a good idea that was to everyone's benefit, especially the seller's, because the margin of profit was hard to beat and a lot of ice cream could be sold in a few minutes in a single large barracks. Following the end of my quarantine, I thus went into the ice cream business during most of my free time. This went on for quite a while, and profits were handsome; like most such things, however, it was too good to last. One day, while I was in an unfamiliar barracks area, a noncom said the captain in charge of that area wanted to see me. So I was conducted to the captain's office, where I followed the appropriate form by coming to attention, saluting, and saying "Sir, Aviation Cadet Brown reporting as ordered." The captain told me to be "at ease" (which was impossible in any meaningful sense, because I was scared to death). Then he explained that I was violating several different regulations, of which the only one I remember was a restriction against buying from a PX and then selling at a profit. He also said that if he reported me to the military police (MPs), I could be arrested and in a great deal of trouble. Needless to say, I believed him and explained I had been unaware of the quoted regulations. So, when he said he didn't want to make trouble but thought I should stop selling ice cream, I assured him I would stop immediately.

At that point the incident seemed to be over, but it wasn't. Upon returning to my own barracks I learned that the sergeant in charge of our area was looking for me, so I went to his office. He said the captain had called and explained he didn't want me to get into trouble but asked the sergeant to call the MPs, get copies of the regulations I was violating, and pass them on to me. The sergeant had already called the MPs and had considerable difficulty getting the regulations, because the MPs were more interested in who had committed the violations. Fortunately, the sergeant finally succeeded without revealing my name.

After I left the captain, he may have wondered if he had frightened me enough, or perhaps thought it his duty to give me the regulations. But he needn't have been concerned. For days afterward I had fantasies about what a close call this had been to ruining my cadet career, and I have always been grateful to that captain for his humane and diplomatic handling of the situation. Thus ended my one and only attempt at free enterprise in the armed forces.

The serious purpose of the classification center at Nashville was carried out after our period of quarantine. A great many physical and psychological tests had been devised to assess the aptitudes of all cadets as pilots, bombardiers, or navigators, and taking these tests required several weeks. The end result was a score in each category and, like many others, I qualified above the minimum level in all three. We were then asked to rank our preferences. Although I had enjoyed my introduction to flying a Piper Cub, I knew that military flying would be very different, and I had no particular desire to become a pilot. But I liked mathematics and had shown an aptitude for it. So I ranked navigator first, bombardier second, and pilot third.

It turned out that two other men, who were going through the classification center in our group, had likewise qualified for all three specialities and given the same rank order of preferences. Shortly before leaving Nashville, we were interviewed together by a captain. Coming to the point immediately, he said: "Now look, you guys, you know as well as I do that we aren't sending anyone to navigator school unless he has a minor physical problem, such as having to wear glasses, which would prevent him from becoming a pilot or bombardier. You aren't in that category. If you insist we will send you to bombardier school, but we'd be much happier if you would be good guys like all the rest and become pilots." I stuck to my guns, so to speak, as did the other two, so we were classified to become bombardiers.

The next phase of our training was Preflight, which lasted six to eight weeks and was attended by all cadets regardless of their eventual specialty. For me, this was at Ellington Field, a major center for Preflight training near Houston, Texas. We were taught Morse code, in which everyone had to attain minimum speeds for both sending and receiving, and aircraft identification was introduced. Physical conditioning was emphasized with daily calisthenics, and we often ran obstacle courses, which tested our strength, agility, and endurance. On one occasion we even bivouacked for several days, the purpose of which was unclear, but the rain and mud certainly tested our tolerance for discomfort.

What I remember best about Preflight, however, was the close-order drill. It was still summer, and the humidity in the Houston area was high. As a result, I clearly remember how the prickly heat felt as it seemed to slither around on my back while we drilled, sometimes in the hottest time of day and in the direct sunlight. However, drill proved more interesting for me than for most because I was appointed a cadet squadron commander. I don't know how the selection was made, nor do I remember any duties other than drilling a squadron of about two hundred cadets, a pleasant assignment that helped take my mind off the heat. I had learned to dance a few years before and enjoyed it greatly, partly because of the excuse to be close to a girl and partly for the challenge of devising dance steps to go with the music. Though close-order drill does not have many steps, I came to think of it as a highly regimented dance and enjoyed putting my squadron of cadets through its paces. It was also fun to be giving orders for a change and to watch about two hundred men executing them, my first experience of that kind of responsibility and satisfaction.

There was little time off in any stage of our training, but in Preflight we got some of our weekend days off to go into Houston by bus. At that time, Houston was just a midsize city with a well-defined main street and town center, which included a USO, the main place of interest to us. Years later, in the 1970s, I was there for the first time since World War II and couldn't even find the Houston I had known.

It had become completely lost in the sprawl, reminding me of nothing so much as Los Angeles.

In Preflight I also became acquainted with the famous Texas pride in everything Texan that is bigger or better than anywhere else. This came about mainly through John Brooks, a bunkmate from Houston who became a good friend. I remember John as a wonderful fellow who spent a lot of time in his bunk. We remained together in gunnery and bombardier schools because of bunk assignments being alphabetical by surnames, and under his picture in the yearbook of our bombardier class he is quoted as saying, "I was born in Houston but I'll die in my sack." Anyway, one day John was lying in his sack looking up at the ceiling (his favorite pose) when suddenly out of nowhere he said, "Did you know the San Jacinto Monument is the tallest in the world?" I said this was surprising because I happened to know that the Washington Monument is five hundred fifty-five feet high. "Oh," he said, "the San Jacinto is five hundred eighty." Another time (but from the same position) he suddenly said, "Did you know Texas has the largest pine tree forest in the world?" I said, "Well, John, you've certainly gone too far this time. What about Siberia?" He looked at me and replied loftily, almost pityingly, "Oh, that's spruce." I never did learn whether John was serious about these things or just spoofing, and maybe it's better that way. But I did learn with some relief that Texans can make fun of themselves. In Houston, the streetcars had advertisements in the coves of their ceilings, and posted there occasionally was a Texas best under the title of "Texas Brags." One of these said, "Texas is the place that has more cows and less milk, more rivers and less water, you can look farther and see less than anywhere else in the world."

My next phase of training was aerial gunnery, because bombardiers sometimes used a .50-caliber machine gun in the nose of a bomber. This took me to Laredo, Texas, for about six weeks. The training there included rigorous practice in aircraft identification, taught mainly by flashing the silhouette of an aircraft onto a screen for only a fraction of a second, after which we were asked to identify it. Both friendly and enemy aircraft were shown, including all types that we were likely to encounter, and each plane was shown head-on, from the side, above, or below. This type of training was very effective, and many cadets attained high scores. It was critically important, so that we wouldn't shoot at friendly planes but would shoot at an enemy plane without hesitation, the decision in aerial combat sometimes being required within a split second.

We also spent much time on the skeet range, using shotguns to shoot at clay targets thrown in various directions from several different locations. This was to help us learn the fine art of "leading" a target by the right amount, depending upon the angle at which it was "flying" in relation to where we were standing, and to do this very quickly and reflexively. All of this was good fun and of obvious potential value. We also learned to strip and reassemble machine guns blindfolded, because this might be required under emergency conditions and even in darkness. Then we fired the guns at stationary targets on the firing range, and for the finale we fired a .30-caliber machine gun from the open rear cockpit of a training plane at a sleeve target towed by another plane. This was all very exciting and made me feel I was getting to the guts of what we were training for.

Toward the end of our gunnery training, John Brooks learned that the Houston Symphony was coming to Laredo to give a concert. He urged me to attend with him and said this would be special, partly because the bassoonist was considered the greatest woman bassoonist in the world. I agreed to go with him but privately wondered just how many woman bassoonists there were in the world at that time. When the evening came, there was a festive air about it, and we attended with considerable anticipation. After the performance, I had to agree with John that the woman bassoonist indeed had a special talent. She was always able to anticipate the exact moment, when the entire orchestra would be briefly silent, to open her sputum valve and blow out the excess sputum. I found this amusing but also a little sad, because thereafter John didn't have quite the same enthusiasm for his stories of Texas greatness.

My final training was in a bombardier school at Midland in western Texas. There I learned to use the Norden bombsight, which was then supersecret and regarded as a wonder, because it permitted bombs to be aimed much more accurately than with any previous method. In principle, it was a mechanical computer, the successful use of which required considerable training and close cooperation between the bombardier and pilot.

Prior to starting a bomb run, the pilot was given an altitude, airspeed, and compass course to fly toward the target during the early part of the bomb run. Also, in preparation for the bomb run, the bombardier subtracted the target's altitude above sea level from that of his plane, to obtain the true altitude of his plane above the target. This altitude was fed into the bombsight, along with the plane's airspeed and the ballistic characteristics of the bombs to be used. All of these were essential for the bombsight to calculate the exact distance before the target at which the bombs should be released. Then the bombardier directed the pilot to a previously chosen initial point (IP), an easily identified point on the ground from which the bomb run began.

Upon reaching the IP, the bombardier began looking through a telescope that was part of the bombsight and that contained crosshairs for aiming. He then used control knobs on the bombsight to center his crosshairs on the aiming point. Much more difficult, he then had to keep the crosshairs riding upon the aiming point, so that the aiming point was being tracked by the telescope. The pilot's initial compass course took into account the expected wind direction and speed in the target area, so that the plane's track over the ground was approximately toward the target. But the winds were never known exactly, so the crosshairs usually drifted off the aiming point to the left or right. This could be compensated for only by altering the heading of the airplane. For this purpose, the pilot's instrument panel contained a pilot's directional instrument (PDI). When the bombardier turned an appropriate knob on his bombsight, the needle of the PDI moved left or right of center. Then the pilot's task was to make a course correction of the appropriate direction and magnitude to bring the needle back to center. This procedure usually had to be repeated several times before the desired course was obtained; hence it consumed much of the time during a bomb run. When performed correctly, the effect of wind drift was exactly compensated for and the plane's course over the ground was directly toward the target. Thus this procedure was known as "killing the drift." The bombardier also had to manipulate a knob to stop any fore or aft movement of the crosshairs from the aiming point. This took much less time and was known as "killing the rate," because it matched the movement of the telescope to the speed of the aircraft over the ground. When the crosshairs were riding steadily upon the aiming point, the bombardier's task was almost complete, but fine last-minute corrections were

21

required in most cases. A moving cursor on the top of the bombsight showed the progress of the plane toward the release point, thus informing the bombardier how much time remained to bomb release, and when this cursor reached the end of its track, the bombsight triggered bomb release by sending an electrical signal to the release mechanism.

We first practiced this procedure on the ground, using trainers that closely simulated conditions during an actual bomb run. They moved on wheels over a concrete floor, upon which aiming points were marked, and each contained a bombsight and an instructor who also acted as the "pilot." Many such trainers were provided, in a huge building used only for that purpose, so that many student bombardiers could practice at the same time.

We then practiced bombing from the air, using a training plane that was crewed by both a pilot and a bombing instructor. West Texas was ideal for bombing ranges, and we used them intensively. An aiming point was provided on the ground, and we dropped dummy bombs containing just enough explosive to show where they hit. There were usually two student bombardiers, each dropping a number of practice bombs during a training flight.

We also learned aerial navigation, first in classroom courses and then by training flights. The methods used were pilotage, which is navigation by visible landmarks, and dead reckoning, which is much more demanding but necessary in poor visibility. In dead reckoning the navigator must determine the wind direction and speed, then compute the compass course the pilot must fly to travel the desired course over the ground. Also, from the airspeed indicator and wind data, the ground speed could be computed, from which the navigator could obtain an estimated time of arrival (ETA) for any given destination. These computations required geometry and elementary mathematics, and we were also aided by a mechanical hand-held instrument known as an E-6B computer. Our training in these basic methods of navigation was as intense and complete as that of cadets trained to become fully rated navigators. But rated navigators also learned celestial navigation, which was sometimes needed for long flights at night or over water. Using our basic methods, we were responsible for navigating any plane to which we were assigned after graduation, so we were often referred to as bombardier-navigators. Indeed, we spent much more time navigating than bombing, because most bomb runs required only a few minutes.

Our bombardier class contained one hundred thirty-eight cadets, and the prescribed length of training was eighteen weeks. But a strange thing happened. Early one morning, about ten days before graduation, a group of about fifteen of us was told we were graduating that day. No one had heard of anything like this happening before, so we couldn't have been more surprised, and it seemed almost impossible to accomplish everything required to graduate that soon. What I remember best was the problem of uniforms. Upon graduation we became second lieutenants, which required custom-made uniforms ordered weeks before. Someone had come to measure all of us, which was critical because our uniforms were supposed to fit snugly without being uncomfortable. As far as we knew, none of these uniforms had been delivered to our base yet. However, by some miracle the uniforms for our small group all showed up that day, and everything fitted perfectly, at least in my case. There was also much processing and paperwork. So we were scrambling furiously throughout the day to finish everything required.

The deadline was a graduation ceremony on the drill field, in the latter part of the afternoon, and we had to appear in our new uniforms. It was quite a sight. With our training officers and most of our class drawn up to attention at the prescribed time, cadets of our small group continued to appear from the barracks and come running across the drill field to join the formation. Finally we were all assembled and the ceremony proceeded, with some very unmilitary halfsmiles and amused sidelong glances.

Early the next morning an army transport plane flew us to MacDill Field near Tampa, Florida. Then nothing happened! Although we had expected to receive urgent assignments of some kind, no one seemed to know what to do with us. In the meantime, we were quartered in tents in Florida's hot spring sun. Finally, we were sent home on leave. At that point, of course, whatever plans had been made for us had obviously been changed.

I have often wondered what those plans were and have thought of only one reasonable possibility. Since atomic bombs were being developed at that time, our small group may have been intended for training and combat experience in B-29s, prior to final selection of the few bombardiers assigned to crews chosen to drop those bombs.

This could explain the initial urgency, including the early graduation of a selected group, and the large effort committed to the original plan. If this hypothesis is correct, our small group of bombardiers had a close brush with history that I am glad became nothing more than that.

Following home leave, the members of our group began to receive orders for operational training in heavy bomber crews (B-17s and B-24s) at Florida air bases. Then one day a notice appeared on the bulletin board that volunteers were being accepted for operational training in B-26 Marauder crews at Barksdale Field near Shreveport, Louisiana. This plane had developed a reputation for being accident-prone and dangerous, which I assumed was the reason they asked for volunteers. On the other hand, I was much more attracted to tactical bombing in medium bombers than to strategic bombing in the "heavies." This was partly because of the more strictly military targets of tactical bombing, conducted in close support of our ground troops, and the feeling that tactical work would be more effective in winning the war as soon as possible. Also, the high altitudes of heavy bombers required crew members to be constantly connected to an oxygen supply and to wear multiple layers of heavy, stiff clothing. These unappealing restrictions did not apply at the medium altitudes of B-26 operations, and with a crew size only about half that of heavy bombers, I anticipated a more cohesive spirit and more room for individual initiative. Finally, and perhaps most decisive, I felt that the B-26 would be a more exciting and adventurous plane in which to serve. So I signed up and was promptly accepted.

Chapter 3

The Martin B-26 Marauder

W hen I arrived at Barksdale Field I knew almost nothing about the B-26 or its early history. For the reader, however, this seems a good place to present those subjects, as background to later aspects of this narrative.

In any discussion of the Martin B-26 Marauder, an explanatory note is required because the Douglas A-26 Invader, in which I served during the last few weeks of the war in Europe, was soon thereafter redesignated the B-26. Two planes are never supposed to have the same designation, but it happened. To avoid this source of confusion for the reader, I will refer to the Douglas Invader only as the A-26, its original designation that applied during World War II.

In 1939 the United States was woefully ill-prepared, especially in the air, for the kind of war being threatened by Hitler. The B-26 was developed to help fill that need, and it became an extraordinary airplane. The specifications sent to aircraft builders seemed impossible to meet with the design experience and construction methods available at that time. These specs were for a twin-engine medium bomber with a speed of 250 to 300 miles per hour, a range of 3,000 miles, a maximum bombload of 4,000 pounds, and a service ceiling of 20,000 to 30,000 feet. In short, although it would have the speed of a fighter plane, its service ceiling and bombload would be typical of the B-17 Flying Fortress, as that famous heavy bomber was used in missions against Germany. Put another way, the B-26 would fly faster, farther, and carry a heavier bombload to greater heights, than any twin-engine aircraft yet built.

This unprecedented challenge was met by Peyton M. Magruder, a twenty-six-year-old aeronautical engineer at the Glenn L. Martin Co. in Baltimore. His project team worked on the design day, night, and weekends, and even so, they met the deadline for bids with only hours to spare. Bid selection was made by assigning points for desirable aspects of the design, and Glenn L. Martin won the contract hands down with a score of 813.6 out of a possible 1,000. The nearest competitor, North American Aviation, scored 673.4 points and was awarded a separate contract, which resulted in the B-25 Mitchell.

Because of the developing war in Europe, the Army Air Forces did not authorize the building and testing of any prototypes of the B-26 but took the first plane off the production line for initial testing. This radical departure from accepted procedures had never before been done for a bomber. In fact, the need was so great and the Army's faith in Glenn L. Martin was so complete that 1,131 B-26s were ordered before the first plane even came off the production line. The contract with Martin was signed in September of 1939, just after Hitler started World War II by invading Poland, and the first plane came off the production line on November 25, 1940, only fourteen months later, just after the Battle of Britain was won. Incredibly, when the first plane was flown, it passed all the tests. In both design and production it thus became something of a miracle. So the B-26 was off to a fine start, breaking precedents and setting records from the very beginning.

In the early stages of using this plane, however, the high losses in training led to the saying "a plane a day in Tampa Bay." The actuality was more like one a week, so this saying was untrue. But it tumbled easily from the lips and made a pleasing sound; hence it clung tenaciously to the B-26. Losses in training were indeed high, however, resulting largely from the lack of prototypes on which to work out the inevitable design and construction bugs, which were discovered only in use after many planes had been produced and flown. This problem was made even more severe by both the advanced design of the plane and the extreme time pressure that prevailed during its design and production. In addition, early instructors and pilots thought of it as such a "hot" plane that they often tried to fly it like a fighter, which had never been intended. So the B-26 also became known as the "widowmaker." Although much of the widowhood resulted from unwise pilots, and though the plane's design was not responsible for the lack of prototypes, that name likewise became so overused that it survives to this day. Thankfully, by the time I began training in B-26s, pilots had become resigned to it being a bomber. But little wonder this initial problem occurred, because it *was* a hot plane. Its approach speed for landing was about 150 miles per hour, with touchdown at about 115, which was higher than the landing speed of any World War II fighter aircraft. In fact, pilots of the time considered even a fighter to be very hot if it landed at more than 70 miles per hour.

The B-26's high stall speed and fast landings resulted from a wing-span of only 65 feet and a gross weight (the maximum allowable fully loaded) of about 34,000 pounds, which produced the highest wing loading (weight carried per unit area of wing) of any combat aircraft at that time. Indeed, the wings were so short that the B-26 was often called "the flying prostitute" because it had no visible means of sup-port. Some of the early B-26 flyboys were so ridiculously proud of this reputation that they clipped the outer feathers from their silver pilot's wings. A high percentage of these "clipped-wing" pilots may have spun in, with or without the aircraft, but history yields no stat-istics on that point. To meet the specs, or even to fly at all with such a high wing loading, required powerful engines, so the B-26 had 2,000 horsepower radial engines and four-bladed propellers (the first used on a bomber) that were 13½ feet in diameter.

Due to its accident-prone initial record and the even worse reputa-tion that resulted, the B-26 almost aborted. This was mainly because Senator Harry Truman, chairman of the Senate Investigating Commit-tee, was concerned about waste in the military. Under his guidance, this committee recommended repeatedly that B-26 production be halted. Fortunately, that was averted, partly by Martin justification reports and probably even more by B-26 pilots flying combat in the Pacific who testified to its fine performance. But the person who did the most to save the B-26 was General James Doolittle, who gave demonstration flights to show its airworthiness, including single engine climbs from just after liftoff, and who did everything else in his power to prevent this plane from becoming extinct. Fortunately, those efforts were successful. I have also heard from several sources that General Doolittle was keen to use the B-26 for his raid on Tokyo. As he says in his autobiography, however, the B-26 could not take off within the 500-foot length of an aircraft carrier, so the B-25 was the only plane available that met all of his requirements. Thus the B-25 became justifiably famous for the audacious Tokyo raid, which undermined Japanese morale by proving their homeland vulnerable to American attack from the air, something their emperor had assured them could never happen.

With time and experience, the bugs were eliminated from both the B-26 and its pilots. Significant design changes also were made that probably would have been introduced earlier in production if prototypes had been made and tested. The original wingspan was used for the early versions (the B-26, B-26A, and the first 641 B-26Bs), then it was increased by six feet to improve lift.

At about the same time, heavier armament was added in response to requests from the Army. The original design provided .30-caliber machine guns, one each in the nose, top turret, tail, and belly, but this firepower quickly proved inadequate. So all machine guns were changed to the much more effective .50-caliber. Also, a newly designed top turret and a newly designed tail turret were installed, each with twin .50s, and four forward-firing guns were mounted on the sides of the fuselage. In the waist, a single belly gun was changed to two guns firing from ports, one on each side of the plane. Only the nose gun was unchanged, except for its increased caliber. Thus the B-26's defensive firepower was greatly increased.

This extra firepower, plus armor plate and other equipment desired by the Army, increased the plane's gross weight to 38,200 pounds. In spite of the longer wing, this extra weight made the wing loading even higher than in the original design. That problem was solved, beginning with the B-26F (there was a B-26C but no D or E models). By tilting the leading edge of the wing upward 3.5 degrees, lift was increased enough to bring landing speed down to 135 miles per hour on the approach and about 104 on touchdown. This design change also permitted the use of shorter runways and provided a greater reserve of lift for emergency conditions, such as flying on single engine. Top speed was slightly reduced, but that sacrifice was deemed minor by comparison with the advantages attained. Compromise, which is intrinsic to aircraft design, had been developed to a fine art by Martin engineers. And throughout its production, in addition to major changes that resulted in new models with new letter designations, minor changes were constantly being made in almost every aspect of the plane. So the B-26 became a finely tuned orchestration of compromises that not only met the seemingly impossible initial requirements but provided additional advantages of many kinds.

The most dangerous early problem with this plane was runaway propellers on takeoff. The propeller pitch control was electrical, and when it failed, pitch was quickly lost entirely. At zero pitch, all four propeller blades were in the same geometric plane as the one in which they were being rotated by an engine. Though the propeller then ran away and whirled at high speed, it not only produced zero thrust, but drag was increased. When this occurred just after liftoff, while thrust was most needed and the ground was close, the plane inevitably crashed, killing most or all of the crew. This problem proved to result from the plane's batteries being used for engine warm up before takeoff, which drained the batteries, leaving too little electrical power for pitch control. This was solved by the simple expedient of providing a portable electrical generator, at the hardstand of each plane, to start and warm up the engines. Thereafter, runaway propellers became almost unheard of.

Following these major changes, which were complete when the B-26 entered the European Theater, this airplane proved outstanding in almost every way. Most notably, in combat it was able to sustain heavy damage from flak and enemy fighters and still remain sufficiently airworthy to bring the crews home. Indeed, some cases of this type were almost unbelievable, one of which will be described in Chapter 14. This strength and durability contributed greatly to a combat loss rate in the European Theater of only seven-tenths of one percent, the lowest combat loss rate for any World War II aircraft. This value is obtained by dividing the number of planes lost to enemy action during missions (911) by the number of sorties, defined as single-plane missions flown (129,943).

At least equally important was the quality and training of the pilots. In *Flak Bait*, Devon Francis devotes an entire chapter to the outstanding work of Lieutenant Colonel Millard Lewis, who greatly improved the training of B-26 pilots. His pilots also became more highly selected, with only the top one-third, based on earlier stages of training, being accepted for B-26s. Following these changes, Francis says "They were the best pilots in the Army Air Forces." And these changes were also early enough to contribute greatly to the effectiveness and safety of B-26 operations in Europe.

Unmeasurable but also very important was the B-26's contribution to the high morale and esprit de corps of its aircrews. After all, the plane was the most significant material thing protecting anyone up there with bursting flak or enemy fighters all around, so it was a great comfort to have confidence in it. These feelings of respect and gratitude are still very much alive, as indicated by the dedication in 1995 of a B-26 Marauder International Archive, expected to become the largest military archive in the United States, and possibly in the world, devoted to a single type of aircraft. Established under the auspices of the B-26 Marauder Historical Society, this archive was originally at the University of Akron in Akron, Ohio, but much of it is now located at the Pima Air and Space Museum in Tucson, Arizona.

Unfortunately, the planes themselves have not fared as well. None was flown home from Europe after the war. Instead, both in Europe and America, destruction of the remaining B-26s began almost immediately. Engines and other salvageable items were removed; then the planes were blown apart by demolition charges, and bulldozers collected the scrap metal to be melted down. In 1948 the B-26 was finally declared obsolete, and few of the 5,157 planes that had been produced survived the salvage operation. It was sad indeed that such a historic plane should meet such an inglorious end. To at least one former pilot, it was a shattering experience. In *The Martin B-26 Marauder,* Jack Havener describes watching a newsreel, which in those days were always shown in a movie theater before the movie. He found himself viewing a salvage operation of World War II airplanes, which were B-26s, and he suddenly realized they were destroying the one he had flown. As he tells it, "Already shaken by the sight, I sat bolt upright in my seat and yelled: 'My God! That's my plane!'" Not surprisingly, he was so upset that his wife had trouble calming him down, and they left without seeing the featured movie.

In consequence of this destruction, and inevitable attrition among the few B-26s that somehow survived, only four may be seen on exhibit in the year 2001. The only one restored to flying condition is at Fantasy of Flight, an aviation museum in Polk City, Florida, near Orlando. Complete planes also may be seen at two other locations. One is the Air Force Museum at Wright-Patterson Air Force Base near

Dayton, Ohio, while the other is the French Air Force Museum at Le Bourget near Paris. The fourth exhibit is the nose and cockpit of *Flak Bait* at the Smithsonian's National Air and Space Museum in Washington, D.C. This latter plane flew 202 missions, the record among American bombers of all types during World War II.

Though destruction of most of the remaining B-26s was understandable, surely some planes in the best condition should have been saved for posterity. It is also unfortunate that in 1948, when the B-26 was declared obsolete, its designation was assigned to the A-26. In consequence, I have been told several times of an exhibited B-26 Marauder I hadn't heard about. In every such case to date, the plane in question has turned out to be an A-26 Invader redesignated as a B-26.

Something else rankles, however, as equally or more unjust. During the B-26's early history it was rightly called "controversial." However, by the time it began operating in the European Theater, there was no longer any significant controversy. Of course, we still joked about the plane, but I can't recall hearing anything actually derogatory from anyone who served in it. Indeed, it performed so well that our feelings were admiration, respect, and even affection. Nonetheless, the B-26 is still being characterized as controversial, although the perpetuation of that trivializing description is unfair and hurtful to all who designed, built, maintained, and flew the aircraft through its early troubled times. Instead, it should be emphasized that the B-26 was conceived in adversity, then prematurely born to war after a highly accelerated gestation. The people involved were thus confronted with great difficulties, but their efforts carried the plane through all those early obstacles, an admirable achievement that deserves unqualified, and unstinting, recognition.

During the six months between Pearl Harbor and the Battle of Midway, the Japanese moved quickly and efficiently through much of the Pacific, using their large naval force, including carriers. Their navy swept the seas, and their planes swept the air above land and sea, while their army performed conquests with naval assistance. Their victories provided access to vast oil fields in the East Indies and their air-launched torpedoes made short work of both *Prince of Wales* and *Repulse,* Britain's two largest battleships, effectively ending British sea power in that part of the world.

Ducemus!—We Lead! No motto was ever more appropriate than that of the 22d Bombardment Group. At dawn on December 8, 1941, the day after Pearl Harbor, this unit began a journey with fifty-four Marauders—including fifty-two of the first built—from Langley Field, Virginia, to Muroc Field near Los Angeles. After about two months of patrol duty on the West Coast of the United States, to give warning of an anticipated Japanese invasion force, the group moved to Australia, where it established a new headquarters at Garbutt Field, near Townsville on the northeastern coast of Queensland. The 22d was the first complete air group sent by the United States to any combat theater overseas.

To conduct a combat mission, it was necessary to fly north to Seven-Mile Strip, a primitive advance base at Port Moresby in Papua New Guinea, refuel, then perform the mission itself. Operating in this way, they flew the first B-26 mission of World War II on April 6, 1942. This mission was against shipping at the key port of Rabaul, a heavily defended Japanese bastion on New Britain Island, where they sank a transport with the loss of one plane and a crew member to antiaircraft fire. By the end of May, they had attacked Rabaul sixteen times, at a cost of four B-26s shot down and six others destroyed in crash landings. In addition to shipping, their targets were nearby airfields, storage depots, and ammunition dumps. Operations of this type were thereafter conducted frequently and effectively and proved an important factor in stopping the Japanese advance through that area, thus saving Australia from a strong threat of invasion.

In *The Ragged, Rugged Warriors,* Martin Caiden provides a richly detailed description of the 22d's Australian operations, based largely on interviews with surviving members of that group. The day-to-day life was a nightmare of problems that included unbearable heat, voracious mosquitoes, and the necessity of scrounging for everything, including food and clothing. Ground crews and aircrews alike had the additional problem of maintaining the planes despite an extreme scarcity of spare parts and not nearly enough replacement planes to make up for the attrition. Each mission from Garbutt Field to Rabaul took thirty-six to forty-eight hours, of which eighteen were spent in the air. Thus, fatigue from long hours of work and little sleep became a constant condition, and exhaustion was common. The airfield at Port Moresby was in a malaria-infested jungle, with no adequate living quarters, so the crews slept under the wings of their airplanes, using mosquito netting and minimal bedding brought along from Australia. But little sleep was to be had because the airstrip was being bombed or strafed at any time of the day or night. Thus, crews had to be constantly on the alert to get their planes into the air before they were destroyed or damaged on the ground. Their only warning was when enemy planes were first heard, so the crews usually had only about three minutes to get into the air, often with cold engines and a crew chief or radio operator as copilot. In spite of all these hardships, morale remained remarkably high, and during the entire six months between Pearl Harbor and Midway, the only unit that kept hitting the Japanese again and again was the 22d Bombardment Group with its B-26s.

Bombing attacks were made at low altitudes, usually a thousand to fifteen hundred feet. The bombsight employed was the D-8, primitive by comparison with the Norden bombsight used later in Europe, but adequate for low altitudes. Fighter support was very rare, though the 22d was often attacked by Zeros, and four B-26s often held off as many as twenty Zeros. The number of bombers in a mission was usually three to six, twelve at most, and sometimes only one. But the Zero was there in large numbers, and it was the most dangerous fighter plane in the air at that stage of the war. With its high speed, unbeatable rate of climb, and unexcelled maneuverability, no Allied fighter at that time could match it in a one-on-one dogfight. Getting on its tail would result in a tighter turn than the Allied fighter could follow, which quickly placed the Zero, with guns blazing, behind the Allied plane. This usually ended the dogfight, because the Zero could follow almost any evasive maneuver, and its armament included a pair of 20mm cannon firing explosive shells. In addition, during that early stage of the war, the Japanese fighter pilots were talented, highly trained, and extremely aggressive. And three of Japan's top fighter aces of the war were based at Lae, a frequent target of the 22d on the northern coast of Papua New Guinea. This included Hiroyoshi Nishizawa, who became Japan's ace of aces with 102 kills, and Saburo Sakai, their top ace who survived the war, with 64 confirmed air kills. Allied fighter pilots learned to overcome this dangerous combination of plane and pilot only by adopting the hit-and-run tactics developed by General Claire Chennault during his experience with the Zero in China before World War II.

Flying without fighter cover against the formidable Zero would have been utter suicide in any other bomber of that time, but the B-26 usually took it in stride. When attacked by Zeros, the pilots usually went for broke by shoving the throttles forward and diving to just above the water. This produced speeds well above three hundred miles per hour, which the Zero could barely match, leaving the fighter little or no opportunity to maneuver for an effective attack. Also, flying close to the water protected the vulnerable belly of the plane and permitted gunners firing from the top turret, tail, and nose guns to mount a defense. Even when planes were heavily damaged by antiaircraft and/or fighters, they often remained flyable. Thus the B-26's high speed and durable construction often made the difference between survival and disaster.

In some cases, the B-26 pilots even used tactics similar to those of fighter planes. In *Samurai*, a postwar memoir, Saburo Sakai expresses strong admiration for both the B-26 and its pilots. And he says at least one pilot could fly the B-26 like a fighter. This was probably Walter A. Krell, considered by many to be the top pilot of the 22d. For example, on June 9, 1942, only a few days after the Battle of Midway, he survived a head-on suicide attack by Nishizawa, who had become enraged at failing to shoot down any Marauders. In *The Mission*, by Martin Caidin and Edward Hymoff, Krell is quoted as saying "I always forced the Zero pilots to break away in any head-on run like this one.... But something...set an alarm bell clanging in my head. I don't know why; I just knew that this was one Japanese pilot who would play this thing out to a head-on collision." So at the very last moment, giving Nishizawa no time to react, he dived violently under the Zero, which barely missed him. Then, being just over the water, he had to pull violently back on his yoke to return to level flight.

Standing behind Krell in the cockpit was a member of the three-man group sent from Washington to study conditions in the 22d and recommend ways to improve them. During Krell's maneuver this man was first hurled so hard against the top of the cockpit that his neck could easily have been broken, then thrown equally hard to the floor. He was Lieutenant Colonel Samuel E. Anderson, representing the Army Air Forces, who later commanded the Bombardment Division of the Ninth Air Force in Europe and finally retired as a 4-star general. So it was fortunate indeed for the Allied cause that Krell saved him from Nishizawa and that his neck was not broken in the process.

Another member of the three-man group was Lyndon B. Johnson, who represented the Navy, and much later became our president.

Experience of the 22d proved very useful and led to modifications of the B-26. Its initial firepower was based on .30-caliber machine guns, which soon proved inadequate. Instead of requesting modifications on replacement planes that could arrive only much later, many changes were made on the spot. Since conditions were primitive to say the least, these were marvels of improvisation carried out by armorers and aircraft mechanics. Though the nose was not strong enough to absorb the recoil of a .50-caliber machine gun, the necessary bracing was designed and installed along with the larger gun. And "package guns" were installed on either side of the fuselage, near the well for the nose wheel. Like the guns on a fighter plane, these were aimed and fired by the pilot. Some crews even cut openings on either side of the plane, aft of the bomb bay, and mounted .50-caliber guns there. Their creativity proved so sound that most of their modifications were incorporated into later production models.

At that time, when only the short-wing models were available, some pilots still grumbled about the plane and thought of it as a killer. But Caidin found that most, including all of the best pilots, were already fanatically devoted to the B-26—so much so that when headquarters inquired whether they were having serious trouble with it, they replied, in effect, "Yes, we need more of them."

The 22d Bombardment Group flew 147 missions during its first nine months in combat. It was claimed that 94 enemy fighters were shot down, while only six B-26s were lost to fighters during aerial combat. Unconfirmed claims of fighters shot down are often much too high, and that may apply here, but reported B-26 losses are probably accurate. If so, losses to fighters were incredibly low, especially in view of the numerical superiority of the Zeros. Enemy anti-aircraft fire claimed 14 other planes. Dividing the 20 planes lost by the number of sorties (841), combat losses in the air were 2.38 percent, the heaviest of any Marauder group during World War II. However, seven other planes were lost on the ground to enemy bombing or strafing. And no fewer than 37 planes were lost to causes other than combat, such as weather, mechanical failure, and shortage of fuel. The greatest loss of all, however, was 114 men, who were surely among the bravest and most indomitable ever to walk upon, or fly above, this earth.

While statistics can be of interest, let us also listen to Martin Caidin: "Bold, clean, swift, deadly—the Martin B-26 Marauder. Also demanding of her pilots...the men of the 22d Bomb Group loved her—and flew one of the greatest combat records of all time in this airplane."

Most of those men have now departed to lead elsewhere, and I can only add, God bless them all.

The Battle of Midway was a crucial turning point in World War II, to which B-26s contributed in such a unique and highly significant way that it merits special coverage. Though this battle has been described and analyzed in great detail, the critical role of B-26s has remained little known. It appears clearly, however, when the effects of B-26s in that battle are focused upon.

In early May 1942, the Battle of the Coral Sea was fought to a draw, our first in the war with Japan, but nowhere had the Japanese been beaten decisively. As Admiral Chuichi Nagumo's striking force approached Midway on June 4, 1942, with four carriers, two battleships, three cruisers, and eleven destroyers, backed up by other carriers and major vessels in two nearby naval units, the Japanese held overwhelming superiority and had every reason to be confident of the outcome. However, they did not reckon with the brilliance and dedication of American codebreakers.

Japanese naval codes based on the famous Enigma machines had already been broken, and much of their mail was being read. At Pearl Harbor the codebreaking unit was headed by Commander Joseph Rochefort. From decoded messages, his unit knew the Japanese were planning a major attack soon and that their code name for the target was AF, but the target designated by that code name was unknown. So Rochefort proposed a brilliant ploy. He suggested, and Admiral Chester Nimitz approved, that our forces on Midway send a message in plain English reporting that their facilities for making freshwater had broken down. Only two days later a coded Japanese message, stating that AF was running low on freshwater, was intercepted. Thus the place and approximate time of the attack became known, and American naval forces were there to meet it.

Defenses against an invasion were greatly strengthened on Midway, including additional antiaircraft guns and at least fifteen B-17 heavy bombers. During the battle at least six separate group attacks were made by the B-17s upon the Japanese fleet. Although many hits were claimed on carriers and other ships, no direct hit was ever confirmed by either American or Japanese sources. For example, on June 6 a flight of six B-17s dropped twenty one-ton bombs and claimed to have sunk a Japanese cruiser in only fifteen seconds. However, their target proved to be *Grayling,* an American submarine that fortunately escaped without damage by crash diving. In fact, the high altitude of B-17 operations made it almost impossible to hit rapidly zigzagging enemy ships, and the Japanese took full advantage of evasive action. But even a stationary ship, with its relatively narrow beam, would have been a difficult target from B-17 altitudes of about four miles. In addition, being directly over their targets and so high, it was extremely hard either to identify ships or to distinguish between a direct hit and a near miss. So the fault was not with the B-17 crews but with the conditions under which they were required to operate during the Battle of Midway.

Almost as an afterthought, B-26s also were brought to Midway, where a flight of four planes landed on May 29, six days before the battle began. Led by Captain James Collins, the other pilots were Lieutenants James Muri, Herbert Mayes, and William Watson. Muri and Mayes were attached to the 22d Bombardment Group, while the other two crews were attached to the 38th, another B-26 group that had moved in May to new airfields in Papua New Guinea, New Caledonia, and Fiji. Muri vividly recalls what transpired. The four crews had picked up new planes at Hickam Field in Hawaii, planning to fly them to Australia as much-needed replacements, when they became shanghaied into a rendezvous with destiny. All four planes were sent to Pearl Harbor, where naval officers showed the crews some large torpedoes, the first Muri had ever seen. One of these was slung under the belly of each plane, and the crews practiced takeoffs and landings, but no practice runs or drops were attempted before the B-26s departed for Midway, and the pilots were told nothing of what they would be expected to do there.

The battle opened with a bombing raid upon Midway's defenses by Japanese carrier aircraft. The results disappointed the Japanese because antiaircraft defenses were stronger than expected and no aircraft were found to destroy on the ground. This was because American patrol planes had sighted Admiral Nagumo's striking force, and American land-based planes had all been ordered into the air.

This included six U.S. Navy torpedo bombers (TBF Avengers) and the four B-26s armed with torpedoes, all of which were proceeding unescorted to attack the Japanese carriers. Just before going into battle from Midway, Muri says the B-26s were given the course and distance to "a target" and also the target's coordinates, but not even a suggestion of what the target might be. As stated by historian Walter Lord in *Incredible Victory*, "No greener torpedo plane pilots ever flew a mission..." Indeed, they were pickup crews being asked to perform an almost impossible feat.

On Nagumo's flagship, the carrier *Akagi*, was Captain Mitsuo Fuchida, the naval pilot who had led the air attack upon Pearl Harbor. At Midway he was recovering from an emergency appendectomy and could only watch the engagement from the bridge, where he was joined by Admiral Kusaka, Nagumo's chief of staff. After the war, Fuchida's observations were reported in *Midway: The Battle That Doomed Japan: The Japanese Navy's Story* by Mitsuo Fuchida and Masatake Okumiya. Also, Admiral Kusaka was interviewed in Japan by Walter Lord. So eyewitness accounts of what occurred are available from both Japanese and American viewpoints. Of course the full significance of B-26s at Midway could not be assessed until after the war, when Japanese reaction to the B-26 attacks finally became known.

As the American planes approached the Japanese fleet, intense antiaircraft fire and Zeros destroyed five TBFs and one of the B-26s. The surviving TBF, piloted by Ensign A. K. Earnest, released its torpedo at a light cruiser among the screening vessels. Though his plane was badly damaged, Earnest managed to return to Midway with his turret gunner dead and both himself and his radioman wounded. But the B-26s were much harder to stop because of their speed and durability. So the remaining three continued, aiming for the lead carrier, and released their torpedoes. Two of these were headed for *Akagi*, but the torpedoes were slow and the carrier took evasive action, resulting in one torpedo passing on either side. Indeed, postwar reports covering the entire battle reveal not a single hit from American air-launched torpedoes, whether dropped by land- or carrier-based planes.

After dropping his torpedo, Muri continued on, passing low over *Akagi*'s deck from bow to stern, his bombardier strafing all the way with the nose gun. This gunfire killed two men, cut the transmitting antenna, and knocked out an antiaircraft gun. Then the Japanese were given an even greater scare. Fuchida and Kusaka watched in horror as a B-26 hurtled straight toward *Akagi's* bridge. The plane appeared certain to crash there and they thought they were done for, but it finally veered just enough to miss before plunging into the sea. In Fuchida's words, this plane "...skimmed straight over Akagi, from starboard to port, nearly grazing the bridge. The white star on the fuselage of the plane, a B-26, was plainly visible." Kusaka watched it head straight for them and, expecting a collision, reflexively ducked. Walter Lord identifies Herbie Mayes as the pilot and reports that "A shaken Kusaka found himself strangely moved. He thought only Japanese pilots did things like that. He had no idea who this steadfast American was, but there on the bridge of the *Akagi* he silently said a prayer for him." So the Japanese, who had been confident no plane could penetrate their defenses, were greatly impressed by these planes and the valor of their crews.

Collins escaped the Zeros by climbing rapidly into cloud cover at high altitude. Muri tried to do the same but was too heavily beset with Zeros, so he returned to Midway very close to the water, to complete an incredibly harrowing mission. Upon nearing the Japanese fleet, Muri had first realized what the target might be when he saw Zeros circling high overhead in the distance. Soon thereafter, every antiaircraft gun in the Japanese fleet was firing, as were the medium and large guns, including 16-inch guns on the battleships. The big guns could not be aimed effectively at planes, so they were aimed instead at the water just ahead of the planes, causing solid columns of water to erupt upward into the air. The attacking planes were flying just over the ocean surface, and hitting one of the man-made water-spouts was like hitting a brick wall. That was the fate of one TBF, which exploded into debris and disappeared. Muri flew around the waterspouts, while using maximum speed and skidding wildly to throw off the aim of the Zeros. However, the Zeros were so numerous and determined that they could not be avoided. Thus bullets and 20mm cannon shells were tearing through his plane almost constantly as Muri approached the target. In the top turret, Technical Sergeant Gogoj took the brunt of these attacks while firing burst after burst to defend his plane. His turret was severely damaged, and on three occasions he suffered multiple wounds that forced him out of the turret. Each time he returned to defend the plane as best he could.

The tail and waist gunners fared almost as badly and also reacted heroically.

After dropping his torpedo and heading for *Akagi,* Muri was so low over the water that he had to fly upward to clear the deck during his strafing run. While returning to Midway, the Zeros continued to attack but with less determination. Also, after dropping his torpedo Muri found he could maintain a speed of more than 300 miles per hour, enough to actually outrun the Zeros, in spite of considerable damage to his plane and its propellers. Upon reaching Midway, he knew that the left landing gear was useless, so he cocked his plane to the right for touchdown with only the right main gear and nose wheel. When his plane slowed enough that this attitude could not be maintained, the plane sank upon the shattered left main gear and shuddered violently as it came to a stop. While awaiting help for the wounded, some of the crew counted holes in the plane; but they gave up after five hundred, having examined only one side.

Although the B-26 attack inflicted little damage upon the enemy, the qualities of these planes and their crews proved critical to the outcome of the battle. The leader of the Japanese bombing of Midway, Lieutenant Tomonago, had reported failure to destroy any land-based planes on the ground and had recommended a second bombing attack of Midway before attempting an invasion. This was a difficult decision for Nagumo, who was holding back planes armed with torpedoes and armor-piercing bombs, on both *Akagi* and *Kaga,* in the event American naval forces proved to be nearby. Fuchida reports that immediately following the attack by American land-based planes—most notably the B-26s, which had made such a strong impression—Admiral Nagumo ordered the arming of planes on both carriers to be changed for another attack on land targets with fragmentation and incendiary bombs. As Fuchida describes it, "Admiral Nagumo needed no further convincing that Midway should be hit again.... Consequently, at 0715, just as the torpedo attack was ending, he ordered the planes of the second wave, which had been armed for an attack on enemy ships, to prepare instead for another strike on Midway." In *Climax at Midway,* an authoritative account of the battle, Thaddeus Tuleja evaluates Nagumo's decision in an italicized comment (his only one): *"This is the most critical decision of the battle."* Needless to say, such a change of arming on an aircraft carrier is complicated, difficult, and time-consuming. And during that crucial period Nagumo learned from a patrol plane of the dangerously near American naval force. At that point he was forced, in self-defense, to order a second change of arming—back to torpedoes and armor-piercing bombs for attacking ships.

The resulting chaos on the two Japanese carriers can only be imagined. Sporadic attacks upon the Japanese carriers over the next few hours did little direct damage but kept the crews busy, preventing them from properly stowing discarded ammunition. Fuchida describes how crews, who had been furiously replacing torpedos with bombs, now "...hastily unloaded the heavy bombs, just piling them up beside the hangar because there was no time to lower them to the magazine. There would be cause to recall and regret this haphazard disposal of the lethal missiles when enemy bombs later found their mark in *Akagi.*" Furthermore, their highly effective fighters were strained. After a last devastating attack upon the American carrier-based torpedo bombers, the Japanese fighters remained too low over the water to provide protection for their carriers, whose decks were crowded with planes being refueled and readied for takeoff, amid stacks of bombs and torpedoes lying in the open on both flight and hangar decks. Thus, moments later, when American dive-bombers came screaming down upon them, the carriers were at their most vulnerable, and hits from the bombers were quickly transformed into ship-sinking infernos. During five spectacular minutes the tide of war in the Pacific turned in favor of the United States, and it never reversed. In analyzing this fiasco from the Japanese point of view, Fuchida and Okumiya, in *Midway: The Battle That Doomed Japan,* appropriately conclude, "The apparently futile sacrifices made by the enemy's shore-based planes were, after all, not in vain."

This long day of battle sent four Japanese carriers to the bottom, three of which were mortally damaged during the furious first five minutes of action by U.S. Navy dive-bombers. The American carriers involved were *Enterprise, Hornet,* and *Yorktown.* Following severe damage in the Battle of the Coral Sea, the *Yorktown* had been miraculously repaired at Pearl Harbor in only three days to render it serviceable for the anticipated battle at Midway. Sadly, it was sunk before that battle was over, but it was the only American carrier lost. So the carrier score was four to one, indeed an "incredible victory" for the underdog and "the battle that doomed Japan," or at least put an end to her overreaching ambitions for conquest at that time.

In the Aleutian Islands, the Japanese also attacked a U.S. base at Dutch Harbor, on the island of Unalaska, as a diversion to their attack upon Midway. Even at this early stage of the war, preparations had been made for aerial defense of the Aleutians. In May 1942, the 73d and 77th Bombardment squadrons were sent to Cold Bay and Umnak, bases near Dutch Harbor. Initially equipped with seventeen Marauders, they were assigned to patrol offshore waters and attack any Japanese ships sighted, using low-level approaches with torpedoes and skip bombing.

Like the 22d Bombardment Group in Australia, men of the 73d and 77th lived and worked under miserable conditions, with no replacements, difficult maintenance conditions, and inadequate provisioning. Missions were of shorter duration than in the South Pacific, but the weather was even worse. With the pilots encountering severe icing conditions, almost constant fog, and the famous Aleutian "williwaws"—winds so unpredictable that a plane could start takeoff in a headwind and have a tailwind before leaving the ground—flying was not only difficult but unusually dangerous. So the 73d and 77th Bombardment squadrons pioneered with the B-26 at the low end of the temperature scale.

On June 3, 1942, the day before the Battle of Midway began, an enemy task force with two small carriers approached the Aleutians under cover of rain and fog and launched an aerial attack that damaged the U.S. base at Dutch Harbor. Although B-26s searched all that day, they found no enemy ships in the heavy weather. The next day, three planes found targets and launched their torpedoes, all of which missed. The Japanese task force withdrew under cover of darkness but later landed small forces on Attu and Kiska, outer islands of the Aleutian chain.

American torpedoes at that time were apparently too slow, hence easily avoided by evasive action. During early phases of World War II, the firing mechanism also proved sadly deficient on both air- and water-launched torpedoes. It must have been the ultimate in frustration to watch a torpedo strike the target but then fail to explode, especially when the torpedo was launched after great effort or even sacrifice. Thus B-26s stopped using them, having much better success with bombs.

On October 12-13, B-26s used low-level attacks and skip bombing to hit and beach two Japanese transports at Kiska. Then, on October

16, six Marauders sank a destroyer and heavily damaged another. Next, four B-26s attacked and reportedly sank an 8,000 ton Japanese freighter near Attu on Thanksgiving Day, and on December 11 another transport was sunk near Kiska. Only two planes were downed by the enemy during these attacks, both by antiaircraft fire from destroyers, but thirty more were lost to "other causes" while serving in the Aleutians. By January 1943 the 73d and 77th squadrons were converted to B-25s, and in August of that year the Japanese withdrew from Attu and Kiska.

Marauders also participated in other actions in the Pacific Theater, such as the battle of Guadalcanal, where the United States first used amphibious assault to recapture territory taken by the Japanese. The B-26s provided air cover by watching for Japanese ships as the invasion fleet approached Guadalcanal on August 5 and 6. They also hit Japanese airfields at Rabaul in Papua New Guinea, where they destroyed planes on the ground and put runways out of action, thus preventing Japanese bombers from disrupting the American landing on Guadalcanal. After storming ashore at Guadalcanal on August 7, U.S. Marines took an important airfield that the Japanese had built. Renamed Henderson Field, it was then used by American air-craft—including Marauders—to complete securing of the island. Marauders assisted by bombing and strafing ahead of Marine lines, and they also attacked enemy ships sent to support the defenders, with one such vessel reported sunk.

Here, I have only cited highlights of B-26 contributions in the Pacific, with the intent of providing the reader with an overview. Other works are available for details, and a vivid account of B-26 operations in all theaters of World War II is provided in a video titled *The B-26 Marauder in Action*.

During 1943, Marauders in the Pacific were steadily replaced by B-25 Mitchells, and the last B-26 sortie in that theater of war took place on January 9, 1944. Though the thinking behind that policy may never be known, two factors were probably decisive. Since B-25s could use shorter runways than B-26s, the former were better suited to the Pacific War, especially as our forces island-hopped closer to Japan and many new runways had to be built. Meanwhile, B-26s were proving almost ideal for the Mediterranean and European theaters. Hence all available Marauders were being concentrated there, and demand exceeded supply, so it was probably inevitable that B-25s took their place in the Pacific. But this did not occur without protest. General George Kenney, commanding general of the Fifth Air Force in Australia and the Philippines, wrote as follows to USAAF Headquarters in Washington, D.C.: "I know you have set me up for the B-25s but the B-26 is a much better combat job. While the B-26 may be frowned upon in some circles at home, the boys here prefer it to the B-25 every time. The B-26 has a better bomb load, more range, is faster, more maneuverable and stands up much better in a crackup. We will buy [take] all you have. In peacetime the boys would probably prefer the B-25, as it is considerably easier to fly, but when they are shooting for keeps the B-26 takes care of itself and comes home."

Chapter 4

Operational Crew Training

At Barksdale Field I was assigned immediately to a B-26 crew, which consisted of six men. The other five had arrived much earlier and had already done everything they could without a bombardier-navigator. Unfortunately, this hadn't been much, because almost every training flight involved practice bombing or navigation or both. So they had been idle several weeks while waiting for one of the few men completing bombardier school at that time. In consequence, they had become bored and were delighted to see me or *any* bombardier-navigator, so they could get on with their training.

The pilot in our crew was Ken Chapin, who occupied the left seat in the cockpit, while Don Fry was the copilot on the right. I used the Plexiglas nose, where the Norden bombsight was located, for bombing and all navigation that required pilotage. There was also a navigator's workplace, behind the cockpit on the right side, where I navigated by dead reckoning. Three enlisted men had special duties and also served as gunners. John Myers, our radioman, had a workplace to the left of the navigator's position. In combat he was also the waist gunner, using machine guns that fired out of waist doors on either side of the airplane. Bob Graves was our top turret gunner and armorer, who loaded and maintained all the machine guns. Garland Fawcett (better known as Spigot) was our tail gunner and engineer responsible for in-flight maintenance of the aircraft.

Of course, the pilot was in command of the plane and crew, but the atmosphere was mainly that of a team where everyone does his part with little need for orders. They were given, of course, but they didn't need to sound like orders, because the chain of command was understood as a necessary part of our work. By the time we reached combat, we had become comrades-in-arms, a complex relationship I'm not sure anyone has described adequately. We then became even more relaxed with each other, with things like rank and chain of command being respected but taken more lightly. Yet responses to orders were even more disciplined because the stakes were higher and there was often no time for questions or discussion.

The only member of our crew I knew socially during training was Ken Chapin. Coming from a long line of early American pioneers, he had grown up on a farm in Michigan. While in pilot training, his first choice of plane had been the B-24 Liberator, a four-engine heavy bomber. That plane required a minimum height of 68 inches, and Ken was only 66½ inches, so he had been assigned to his second choice, the B-26. Though medium in height, Ken was outsized in other respects, including physical strength and force of personality. A perfectionist by nature, he demanded much of others—but most of all from himself. This, combined with idealism and humor, was the core of his success—both as a pilot and as a person I liked and admired.

At Barksdale most of us lived on the base, in my case in a four-man shack covered with tarpaper. In the Louisiana summer those shacks became incredibly hot during the day and never cooled much during the night. Ken was luckier, or maybe a better planner. In any case, about three months before starting our operational training he married Doloria, his girlfriend of long standing. She moved down to be with him, and they lived in a small cottage off the base. A few times they had me to dinner, which provided one of my most memorable experiences from that period. They had taken a cat and a rabbit for pets, and Ken had told me the animals were so jealous of each other they would eat each other's food. I could hardly believe this, but the first time I visited, Ken tossed some meat on the floor, and indeed the rabbit ate some of it. Then he tossed out a large piece of lettuce, and the cat ate some of that. This has served ever since as a powerful reminder not to underestimate the power of jealousy.

As our pilot, Ken was also the crew member with whom I worked most closely. My navigational instructions were always given to him. Also, on a bomb run with the Norden bombsight, the necessary changes of course were relayed to the pilot by the PDI. Theoretically, when the bombardier signaled for a course correction and the pilot recentered the needle of the PDI, the needle would remain steadily on the center mark, and we would be dead on course for the target. However, it took considerable practice for the pilot to make indicated course corrections without either undershooting or overshooting. To whatever extent he missed, the PDI would soon indicate a further course correction to be made. This coordination between bombardier and pilot was vital, not only for accurate bombing but also for safety of the plane and crew. This was because evasive action to avoid flak was not possible on the bomb run. Accurate bombing required straight and level flying for at least two minutes, and it took only about twenty seconds for a flak shell to reach us at our usual bombing altitude of about twelve thousand feet. So the bomb run was the most dangerous part of most missions, and safety could be improved only by keeping it as short as possible.

Our operational crew training lasted about four months, roughly from April through July 1944. My letters home mention how hard and exhausting this training was. We were being pushed through the program as rapidly as possible, probably because replacements were needed overseas. One letter noted that although it was difficult to get used to bombing from a B-26, I finally became satisfied with our bombing scores. But I was especially pleased with my navigation, and on a 500-mile trip over the Gulf of Mexico we hit our landfall right on the nose. I say "we" because it was a cooperative effort; my compass course could have given that result only if flown accurately and steadily over the entire distance. So I wrote also about our crew—how good it was and how well we got along together.

When Bob Graves came down with appendicitis and was operated upon, I mentioned in a letter how much we all missed him. Doloria went to see him in the hospital and found him climbing the walls for fear of being separated from our crew by the required six-week recovery period. Meanwhile, Ken was tearing his hair wondering how to get rid of an unsatisfactory replacement who had been assigned to our crew. So when Ken learned of Bob's distress, he called our commanding officer, who in turn called the hospital. Upon learning that Bob's condition was "satisfactory," our CO said Bob was needed back in his crew as soon as possible. The hospital agreed, but only if Bob would be assisted getting in and out of the plane, to spare his abdominal muscles while completing his required gunnery practice. Ken agreed, so Bob left the hospital after only about three weeks, thus solving both his problem and ours.

I recall few details of our operational training, probably because we had already learned our specialties and weren't learning much that was really new. Instead, and very important, we were practicing the application of our specialties with smooth coordination within the requirements of a B-26 aircraft. We were also adjusting to each other's personalities and learning mutual trust. With time and practice, we thus became a crew in the best sense of that word.

Chapter 5

The Northern Route to Europe

U pon completing our crew training shortly before August 1, 1944, there was speculation about where we would go into combat. Despite rumors that we would go to India by boat, the situation favored Europe, which proved to be our destination. So we were sent to the Combat Crew Center at Hunter Field near Savannah, Georgia, to be outfitted for the trip. We would fly our own planes, which efficiently transferred a plane and crew together, both of which proved much needed. Unfortunately, while at Hunter Field I contracted the flu. In those days, flu was taken much more seriously than now, so I was hospitalized for more than a week. This delayed our departure and worried me greatly, partly because I felt I was letting the crew down, but I also feared they would be sent without me and we wouldn't get together again. Instead, all the rest of the crew were given three-day leaves, which they didn't seem to mind at all. We finally left together soon after August 10, the date of my last letter home from Hunter Field.

Many B-26s were flown to Europe by a southern route from Brazil to Ascension Island and then to Accra, on the northwestern coast of Africa. In summer a northern route was also open and much used, probably because the shorter overwater flights made navigation less hazardous. The first leg of our trip was from Savannah to Presque Isle, Maine. The only thing I remember from that flight was passing over New York City when there was just one cloud in the sky. But that cloud was small and thin and impaled upon the Empire State Building, like a pancake upon a spit. Most striking and unusual!

The following day we flew the next leg, to Goose Bay, Labrador. Most of this flight was over very lightly populated country. Labrador itself proved especially bleak and barren, but I well remember my night there. We were required to provide security, so each night one of us had to guard our plane, armed with the Colt .45-caliber automatic pistol each of us had been issued. This personal sidearm was kept until the end of the war and was worn on all combat missions, in case we were shot down and needed it to evade capture.

The night in Labrador was my turn for guard duty. This involved spending the entire night with the airplane. We were allowed to sleep, which may have compromised the purpose of guard duty, but I doubt anyone could stay awake the entire night while alone. Also, there were similarly guarded planes nearby, which must have added a lot to the security. While lying upon the concrete hardstand, I quickly had my first experience with voracious sub-arctic mosquitoes, which came in swarms. After a futile period of trying to fight them off, I realized that special measures were required, so I got into my sleeping bag, and while lying on my back, zipped the bag up to my chin. This greatly reduced the exposed skin but made the attack upon my face even more concentrated. Then I remembered that before the trip we had been issued a recently developed mosquito repellent. So I dug it out of a deep barracks bag and applied it liberally to my face. As I lay on my back and watched, against the bright starry sky, swarms of mosquitoes flew traffic patterns only an inch or two above my eyes. I gave thanks for the fruits of science and soon fell asleep, waking in the morning with only a few bites, presumably those that occurred before applying the repellent. Later I learned how lucky I was that the repellent had been so newly developed, because the mosquitoes soon became so accustomed to it that they ignored it almost entirely.

The next day we flew to Greenland, which proved an adventure. We had been briefed that German submarines were in the part of the

Atlantic Ocean we were crossing, and we were ordered to report any sub sightings. I assumed this was just routine and had no expectation of seeing anything, especially since the weather was poor. We were in solid cloud most of the way, and about halfway across we descended, hoping to gain visibility. When we finally broke out of the clouds at a low altitude, imagine our surprise to see a sub just ahead and directly below our course. It was already starting a crash dive when I spotted it, probably having heard us before we broke out of the clouds. In any event, it was beginning to submerge as we passed directly overhead. I gave Chapin the best position fix I could under the difficult weather conditions, and he radioed our sighting report to Goose Bay. We were unable to identify the sub as German or American because of so little viewing time and no training of that kind. Whoever it was, we must have given its crew the fright of their lives. Even if friendly, the sub would have crash dived under those conditions. In that area, however, near our northern convoy route, I should think it much more likely that a lone sub was German. In those waters American subs would be protecting convoys and would seem unlikely to be seeking enemy ships, since none was available aside from an occasional lone sub, which would be almost impossible to find. If it was German, and if we had been trained and armed to attack submarines, we would have had an excellent chance to sink an enemy sub on our first patrol. In any case, we thus entered the combat zone before even reaching Greenland. It was a rare occasion because subs were seldom seen, even by planes that patrolled for them constantly.

We had been warned to approach Greenland very carefully, especially in bad weather. To reach the airfield, we had to identify and then fly inland through Tunugliarfik Fjord, which opens on the southwestern coast of Greenland and penetrates deeply into the rugged coastal area. The fjord itself is fairly straight but terminates in a dead end, from which the land rises rapidly toward the Greenland icecap at a height of about two miles. Fortunately, at the head of the fjord the land directly to the left rises much less rapidly than elsewhere. And there, in one of the most unlikely places on earth for a B-26 to land, was an airfield, which began at the shore of the fjord. Indeed, it began *in* the fjord because pilings had been driven into the water, above which they extended about ten feet, and these pilings constituted the landing end of the runway. So one was forbidden to undershoot the runway upon pain of death. But it was also necessary to use as much of the runway as possible, because its length was minimal for a B-26. The situation was alleviated somewhat by the initial part of the runway running uphill at a considerable grade. However, the runway then passed over the hill and *down* at about the same grade. What a place!

In heavy weather it was impossible to approach this airfield safely unless visual contact could be made with the water near the mouth of the fjord before proceeding inland. As an aid to navigation, a radio station, which put out beams in all four of the cardinal directions, had been established on a small, rocky island just offshore from the fjord. We were instructed to fly in upon the western beam, but not to attempt visual contact with the water until cleared to do so by the radio station. If not cleared right away, we were instructed to fly back and forth on the southern beam at 10,000 feet until clearance was obtained. I will never understand why we were all ordered to fly both north and south on that narrow radio beam at the same altitude of 10,000 feet. A number of planes would probably be doing the same thing, so it was a prescription for disaster, and we nearly filled it.

Upon reaching the radio station, we were in dense clouds and didn't receive clearance for a letdown, so we started flying up and down the southern radio beam at the assigned altitude. There was nothing to see, so I was working from the navigator's compartment behind the copilot. At one point I went forward and crouched for a while between, but just behind, the pilots. I was peering ahead into the clouds, when suddenly another B-26 flashed into view almost head-on and passed directly overhead. At head-on closure speed, and with such limited visibility, it was all over in some small fraction of a second. Neither of the pilots saw it because they weren't looking in the right direction when it happened. And I don't recall any of us hearing it because of the much louder noise of our own engines. It was almost as if we had met a phantom in the clouds, but it was a B-26, all right. I can still see it now. I don't think it could have missed us by more than ten or fifteen feet, and it was the closest we ever came to losing our entire original crew.

Soon thereafter we received clearance to let down, which we did near the mouth of the fjord. While still at a safe altitude we spotted a hole in the clouds below, through which we could see the water. So we descended through the hole, identified our fjord, and proceeded inland at low altitude. The scenery was beautiful but stark and menacing. We had to pass several Y-junctions where other fjords came in from the side, and we had been warned not to take a wrong turn because the secondary fjords were too narrow for a B-26 to turn around. Also, when flying up a fjord with solid cloud cover above, it was very dangerous to try to escape by flying back up into the clouds, because we were surrounded by such rugged country. In spite of the warnings, one B-26 flying into Greenland that day did make a wrong turn up one of the smaller fjords. This provided my first acquaintance with the kind of thing that later became almost routine in combat, where the seemingly impossible was accomplished under conditions of extreme necessity. Somehow that pilot *did* turn around in the narrow fjord and thus escaped disaster.

Our own flight up the fjord was uneventful, and upon reaching the airfield Ken turned left and made a fine landing. I will never forget it, because while still moving at high speed up the inclined initial part of the runway, the final half of the runway was out of sight. So it looked as if we would go over a cliff, and, in spite of the briefing, it took considerable faith to believe there was enough runway ahead for us to stop. Upon reaching the parking area, we discovered several hundred feet of copper wire trailing behind the plane. It was the radio aerial that Ken and Don had forgotten to reel in before landing. A five-pound ball should have been on the end, but it had been left behind, probably when it hit the pilings at the touchdown end of the runway. Ken felt awful about it, but the ground mechanic who met us said breezily, "Don't worry about it. We get two or three like this every week."

After landing, the weather worsened and we were weathered in for three days. The air base provided all the necessities but little else, so we were at loose ends. For many of us, poker became one of the best ways to pass the time. I had learned to play poker and blackjack soon after entering the service, and while overseas there was a lot of time to play these games. In Greenland I was not yet playing much, but some others were. One day I was kibitzing over a group of about eight fellows playing the classic game of five-card draw with nothing wild. In one hand the man I was standing behind was dealt an ace, king, jack and ten—all hearts—plus the ace of spades. Some players would have kept the two aces and drawn three cards. This man threw away the ace of spades and drew the queen of hearts to complete a natural royal flush, the best natural hand in poker and the only one I have ever seen. Then came the anticlimax. No one else had much of any-thing, so he made little from the hand. But what a hand!

We were told it was dangerous to climb in the nearby hills and cautioned (or perhaps ordered) not to do it. But we became bored, and after a while the weather cleared enough to be tempting, so a group of us went climbing. We had no special equipment and only our normal clothing and shoes, but the lower hills around the airfield were free of snow and ice in the summer and didn't appear to require anything special. At one point several of us were going up quite a steep slope, with adequate footholds to seem safe, somewhat like going up a ladder. I was in the lead, and as we neared the top, I came to an area of bare rock that was much less steep. It appeared that if I stood up in a crouch and moved quickly I could walk on up to the top. But after a few steps my foot slipped, throwing me forward upon the rock, and I started sliding without any way of stopping. Fortu-nately, the man behind me was firmly supported, and he put up his hand to catch one of my feet, which he then guided onto a foothold. Without his help there would have been nothing to stop me, and it was so steep below I would almost certainly have been killed. It all happened so fast I only realized later what a close call it had been.

From the foothold I regained control and found a safer route to the top, which we used without further incident. At the top of this hill there was hardly any vegetation, and I only found one plant that might be called a flower. It had a single stalk that looked much like the seed stem of a dandelion, because it supported a ball of pure white fibers. But this was no dandelion. It was existing there under condi-tions very few plants could survive. When I tested the white fibers, they proved so tough I could hardly break them. This impressed me strongly, and I have always remembered that plant as a symbol of the pure whiteness and utter toughness of most things arctic.

The man who almost certainly saved my life on that climb was Lincoln C. Mackay (Mack), a pilot with whom I later flew as lead navigator on three combat missions. Needless to say, I am extremely grateful to him. At the time, however, this incident was such a casual and matter-of-fact part of the climb that I doubt either of us thought much about it. Also, I don't recall that we ever spoke of it later, and my efforts to contact him recently have been unsuccessful. I regret this because gratitude is rarely so well earned. He not only gave me the wonderful life I have led for fifty-seven years since then, but he also saved me from my own foolishness. None of us should have been climbing there without adequate training or equipment and after being warned, and I should not have so thoughtlessly risked so much upon not slipping on that bare rock. I could opine that to take such needless risks is part of youth, and perhaps that is true. However, if one takes risks like that, one had better have the support of someone on a much firmer footing.

The flight from Greenland to Iceland was uneventful, but the takeoff was interesting because we initially went uphill, then steeply downhill into Tunugliarfik Fjord. Also, we had wonderful views of the spectacular and forbidding Greenland icecap and the many glaciers feeding into fjords of the Greenland coastline. After landing at an air base near the village of Keflavik, on the southwestern coast of Iceland, we were again weathered in for several days.

Though we were not supposed to leave the air base, Reykjavik, the capital, was only about a thirty-minute bus ride away, and everyone seemed to be going there. So my last evening I went into Reykjavik for a memorable evening of dinner at a hotel and then the USO for chatting and dancing with the friendly local girls. Everything about the city seemed modern, and the women in the hotel were stylishly dressed. Also, almost everyone I met spoke surprisingly good English. But my strongest memory was of a young woman walking across the hotel lobby. Although I saw her only briefly, the impression she left was indelible. Blond, elegant, and exceptionally beautiful, she walked with a stately but natural grace evocative of a Viking queen. She also looked warm and interesting to be with. Since my impression may have been due mainly to youthful imagination, perhaps it is just as well I didn't meet her, which might have proved disillusioning. But somehow I don't think so.

The following morning we flew to Prestwick, on the southwestern coast of Scotland. At briefing before we left, we learned that a B-24 had crashed that morning just after takeoff, with loss of the entire crew. Then, when we went out to our planes, there was a ground fog so thin it swirled about our ankles as we walked. There had been a recent war movie called *A Guy Named Joe,* in which Spencer Tracy played a pilot who was killed. And the pilot heaven to which he went was depicted just like this, a place where thin clouds swirled around the airmen's feet as they walked. I never saw that kind of ground fog anywhere else, and coming right after the disastrous crash it gave me an eerie feeling. Instead of movies imitating life, life was imitating the movies. This seemed an inauspicious way to start another long, overwater flight, but it proceeded without incident and took us safely to Prestwick, the terminus of the northern route. There we dropped the plane we had flown across to the European Theater of Operations (ETO). Though we had been with this plane for eleven days, some of which were exciting, we had not become attached to it because we knew we were only ferrying it over for another crew to use.

Chapter 6
Northern Ireland

From Prestwick, Scotland, we were sent by boat down the Firth of Clyde and across the North Channel to Northern Ireland. We disembarked at Belfast and then traveled by land to a training base about thirty miles west of Belfast, near the small town of Toome. We must have arrived shortly before September 3, because that was the date of my first letter home since starting our journey. At Toome we received a kind of advanced operational training conducted entirely in classrooms. For example, I remember a vivid lecture from a professional parachute jumper who tried to prepare us for the experience if we ever had to jump under combat conditions. He said we should not be frightened because a free fall was one of the most enjoyable experiences a person could ever have. Indeed, he had found it so addicting he had become a professional exhibition parachutist in civilian life. His description of the silence, peace, and utter bliss of a free fall was initially startling to me, because falling had been prominent in my childhood nightmares. Even so, everything he said was credible and convincing.

We were cautioned that in combat we should enjoy our free fall to the fullest by delaying opening the chute as long as possible, because German fighter pilots sometimes shot parachutists on the way down. It wasn't chivalrous or sporting or even much of a challenge. However, chivalry in aerial combat had passed away during the Spanish Civil War in the moment when Luis Muñoz, a Loyalist fighter pilot, shot to death a parachuting Nationalist pilot whose plane Muñoz had destroyed. Until then such an action had been scrupulously avoided, but once the tradition was violated, it proved difficult to reinstate. The savagery even escalated when a horrible revenge was taken on one of Muñoz's fellow pilots.

Since Muñoz had set the precedent, our best protection was to free fall until only a few hundred feet from the ground. I remember wondering, as I still do, how one could judge that distance without practice. It wasn't too critical because we were also told the parachute would provide all of its deceleration from free fall in the instant it snapped open. We would then hit the ground with about the same force as if jumping from a fourteen-foot height without a parachute, and we were told how to roll upon landing to take up some of the shock. Those fourteen feet sounded pretty high, and I wondered about the effectiveness of trying to roll without training. Indeed, I remember thinking that a combat jump must be interesting but not something to look forward to.

For at least one man, whom I met again after the war, this lecture in combat jumping came together in a memorable way. He had gone to a different B-26 group, and on one mission their plane was so badly damaged the crew had to bail out. He had listened well to our parachuting lecture and was recalling it as he enjoyed a blissful free fall. In fact, he enjoyed it so much that when he finally started paying attention to the ground the trees already looked pretty big, so he pulled the rip cord. Immediately thereafter he took a heavy one-two punch—the first shock from the parachute opening, and the second, only an instant later, from his feet hitting the ground. So he verified what we had been told, having made a theoretically perfect jump, but he certainly called it close.

After the war, I became friends with a former B-17 pilot, Larry Wilcox, who had made a particularly harrowing combat jump. When their plane was badly damaged by enemy fighters and going down, the crew had to bail out but were still at high altitude, something like twenty thousand feet. He knew he should delay opening his chute, with enemy fighters still around, but had the bad luck to fall almost immediately into clouds. Without seeing the ground he had no idea how soon to pull the rip cord, but he managed to wait long enough to break out of the clouds. Unfortunately, however, he then fell into a second cloud layer. That was too much to ask of anyone; he couldn't wait it out a second time, so he pulled the rip cord. When he broke through the second cloud layer and could see the ground, he estimated he was still at about ten thousand feet. Soon thereafter, an Me-109 attacked him.

By alternately pulling on the shroud lines with his left and right hands, he started swinging widely to either side like a pendulum. Also, we had been told how to "slip" a parachute by pulling strongly on the shroud lines on one side, thus dumping most of the air trapped under the canopy and causing the parachute to "slip" to one side as it continued to fall. This was usually done to steer the descent in a parachute, either to avoid something dangerous on the ground or to reach a particular drop zone. Larry now started using it for evasive action, for which it proved effective, mainly because of the sudden faster fall during the sideslip. He said he was sometimes actually climbing the shroud lines to slip the chute as much as possible, and he clearly remembered once, in his desperation, even getting his hands into the material of the canopy.

Using these methods, Larry survived many passes by the Me-109. Fortunately, the high stall speed of the fighter plane prevented the pilot from slowing down enough to follow Larry's evasive actions. Finally, when they were close enough to the ground to be dangerous for the fighter plane, it broke off the attack. So Larry survived by desperate and heroic efforts, but he broke his ankle upon landing and found himself in the backyard of a Gestapo headquarters. Taken prisoner immediately, he was then marched about a mile on his broken ankle before receiving medical aid.

At Toome we also heard lectures on how to evade capture and get back to our own lines if shot down in enemy territory. In a surprisingly large number of cases, parachuting fliers landed in remote enough areas that they were not captured quickly, and under those conditions they often evaded capture successfully. While an evader, an airman was still considered a combatant and theoretically protected by the Geneva Convention rules for combatants. But this could not be relied upon. We were told that if capture were imminent and we had any choice, it was safest to surrender to well-organized military units such as the Wehrmacht, with strong traditions of discipline in following the rules. We were warned to avoid the Gestapo and SS troops at all costs, and civilians were likewise considered very dangerous. This was borne out later when I heard that almost an entire crew from our bomb group was killed by farmers with clubs and pitchforks. Also, I recently interviewed by telephone a gunner from our squadron who had to bail out over enemy territory. He landed on concrete and was disabled by a severely dislocated knee, but was nonetheless attacked by a farmer who tried to kill him with a knife thrust to the belly. He managed to deflect the knife but sustained a leg wound, then killed the farmer with his pistol. Of course, many civilians understandably felt vengeful toward bomber crews. However, I didn't know until recently that civilian attacks on airmen actually became official German policy. Thomas Childers, a specialist in modern German history, says in his book *Wings of Morning* that during the war "...the Nazi government had declared all Allied flyers *Luftgangsters* and Goebbels was now officially urging German civilians to take vengeance on all downed 'terror flyers' wherever they found them."

Shortly after the war, I met a man I had known in training, a successful evader who was undoubtedly helped by the lectures at Toome. He had avoided initial capture and buried his parachute to prevent tipping off the locals that an evader was nearby. Then he made his way west slowly, navigating by a very compact map that was part of an "escape kit" we always carried on missions in a leg pocket of our flying coveralls. This "escape map" was printed in color on both sides of thin silk and showed in great detail the large area in which we might end up having to evade. I kept mine as a souvenir and am still amazed that it could be printed in such detail on both sides of the silk without the printing on one side running through to the other. It was a technical marvel that must have been enormously helpful and even a life-saver for many evaders.

Of course, my acquaintance traveled only at night, hiding every day wherever he could. A choice location was a farmer's barn, into which he slipped before dawn, and after hiding all day in the remotest and safest part of the barn, slipped out again after dark. Food was a major problem, and he had to forage for it. His staple turned out to be sugar beets, which were common in Europe at that time and which he pulled up and ate raw. His travel was very slow, being entirely on foot and at night, with difficult navigation, and having to forage for food along the way while taking great care not to be seen or heard. Consequently, he took several weeks to reach friendly lines.

Regarding safety measures, he described one incident with great clarity. Since it was dangerous to cross a road, he routinely remained hidden for a time, watching and listening for any nearby sentry. On this occasion he had been hidden and silent for about twenty minutes. Thinking this long enough to be safe, he was about to get up and cross the road when a cigarette suddenly flared as it was being lit nearby. This was such a shock he continued to remain still for a long time. Then he carefully crept along the road until far enough from the sentry to feel safe, repeated the waiting period, and finally made his crossing.

Although lectures were an important part of our training at Toome, bombardier-navigators spent most of their time learning a new electronic system of navigation called GEE. It had been developed in England and was first put into practice in the ETO, where it was very helpful during the last winter of the war, which had an abundance of bad weather. In principle, this system was similar to current methods of terrestrial navigation that employ signals from three satellites hovering over the earth.

Signals for the GEE system were sent out by three different ground stations, and an airborne navigator was supplied with a cathode ray tube (CRT), the basic instrument later developed much further for TV and many other uses. The navigator could tune in any desired pair of ground stations and measure accurately the time lapse between arrival at his airplane of short pulses sent simultaneously from the two stations. This will be referred to as a time lapse signal (TLS). He then referred to a special map that showed, for a given value of TLS, the curved line upon the ground above which the receiving aircraft would be located. Since the value of TLS could vary greatly, there was a family of these lines upon the map. For ready identification, the TLS lines from a given pair of ground stations was color-coded, and each line was labeled with its TLS value. Put another way, for each pair of ground stations the map showed a whole set of color-coded lines representing various TLS values, something like an array of contour lines. Signals from the ground stations could be paired in three different ways, so there were three sets of TLS lines, with each set having its own color code. This information was overlaid upon a conventional map of Europe. Thus, the navigator could identify a TLS line above which he was located and see exactly where that line lay upon the map. He could then pick another pair of ground stations, whose TLS lines intersected the first set of lines as perpendicularly as possible. By measuring the TLS value from this second pair of stations, he could identify a second TLS line above which he was located. The intersection of those two TLS lines would be the point on the ground above which he was flying. Thus the GEE system provided, for the first time, an electronic method of determining the location of an airplane, even in bad weather when it was impossible to see the ground.

This system was accurate enough that it could also be used in bad weather for bombing relatively large targets, such as airfields, which did not require pinpoint accuracy. In that case a navigator, acting as the GEE operator in the lead plane, first determined the exact values of two TLS lines that intersected over the target. He then set one of these TLS values into the GEE box (as we called the CRT) and directed his pilot by intercom to fly that TLS line toward the other one. This was done by watching a cursor on the GEE box that showed the position of the plane relative to the preset value of the TLS line to be flown toward the target. The bombs had to be released somewhat before reaching the TLS line that crossed the flight path, because the bombs continued to move forward, by inertia, while in the air. So the GEE navigator computed an adjustment, based mainly upon the plane's speed and altitude above the target, to obtain the TLS value of the bomb release point. The progress of the plane toward the preset release point was also shown by a moving cursor on the GEE box, and when the cursor reached the release point, the GEE navigator signaled the bombardier by intercom for immediate "bombs away."

We were not in Northern Ireland very long, only about three weeks, so we didn't have much time for recreation. But I enjoyed what little we had. Everyone seemed to have bicycles, which helped in getting around the sprawling training base. More important, a bicycle was perfect for touring the countryside in our spare time. The turnover of personnel was high, so bicycles were constantly being bought and sold. They were much used but serviceable, so I bought one right away for a few pounds and sold it before leaving for about the same amount, which was how the system worked in most cases.

This was my first chance to see the countryside in the United Kingdom and I made the most of it, either alone or with Ken Chapin. I still have pictures of us picking blackberries in the hedgerows, impressive piles of stone cleared from the fields long ago and over-grown with all kinds of shrubbery. These acted as very effective fences between adjacent fields and served as visible reminders of the extreme difficulties such hedgerows had posed for our troops in Normandy, especially when these strong barriers were heavily defended. So once again I was grateful to be serving in the air.

Most of all, however, the Irish countryside was beautiful and almost all the buildings looked old and historic. Thatched roofs, for example, were still common enough that after a while they were no longer surprising. So I wrote to my parents that "there is a feeling of history in the very air." I found the people on isolated farms especially interesting, very strong and hardy, with roots so deep in the soil I could almost imagine they had sprung from it, like their crops.

I went into Belfast once or twice in the evening, probably on weekends, but remember only one thing from those occasions. We had been warned about what a tough town it was and that we should never walk alone because of the danger of being knocked over the head and robbed. What they hadn't told us, and which much impressed me, was that even the policemen always walked in pairs. I had never seen this before, because at that time foot patrolmen in the United States, to my knowledge, always patrolled alone. How times have changed!

On at least one occasion, we were allowed off the base for an entire day. Ken Chapin and I had heard of a fine Norman castle on the coast about twelve miles north of Belfast, so we traveled there by bus and spent the whole day. The name of the castle, and also the town asso-ciated with it, was Carrickfergus. This undoubtedly stems from medi-eval times, when there was always a nearby town that housed the tradespeople and shops providing services needed by the castle.

When we reached the castle it was some time before we could rouse anyone. But we finally found the caretaker, an old man who was quite knowledgeable about the place and who gave us a fine conducted tour. Clearly, the castle wasn't being seen much in those days, because we were the only visitors.

We were told this was the finest example of a Norman castle still in existence. Its excellent state of preservation was indeed surprising, because it had been built in the twelfth century, not long after the Norman invasion. Ideally situated for defense, it stood at the tip of a small peninsula, hence surrounded on three sides by ocean, and protected on the fourth side by a moat. If an attacking force got over the moat and the outer wall, it would find itself in a large, grassy area extending all the way around the castle. Then, as I recall, the attackers would have to get over a second inner wall to reach a second large, grassy area, which surrounded the castle keep, the defensive core of the castle to which its defenders retreated, if all else failed, for their final defensive action. I remember especially that the stone stairway up through the castle keep, which was several stories high, wound upward in a spiral that turned continuously to the right. We were told this was so right-handed defenders would not only be above the attackers, but also would have space to make free use of their sword arms. An attacker, on the other hand, would have to cross his right sword arm over his head in an awkward position to bring his sword to bear upon a defender above him. This looked like good military design for its time. However, the history of war has been such a constant progression of measures and countermeasures, I can't help wondering whether attackers in those days didn't save an elite corps of left-handed swordsmen for the final attack on the castle keep.

Another memorable feature of this castle was its great hall, which we were told was the best surviving example of that feature of a Norman castle. This one was in an upper story of the castle with a magnificent view, and its size was impressive. I remember it as about thirty feet wide and fifty long, with the ceiling supported by a stone arch extending the full length of the room. Apparently it was used only for special occasions. And what events they must have been! It was easy to imagine the kind of bacchanalian revels that must have taken place there, and imagination was probably the best way to enjoy them, because the real thing would probably be disgusting by modern standards.

Upon completing our training at Toome, we traveled by boat to England and then took a train to Matching Green, an air base between London and Cambridge. There we joined the 572d Squadron of the 391st Bombardment Group. This bomb group had been at Matching Green since January 1944, having flown its first mission on February 15, then operated intensively to prepare for and support the D-Day invasion. In consequence, although the tour of combat missions in B-26s was sixty-five, many crews were already completing their combat assignments and going home, so we were needed as replacements.

For us, it was a privilege and a great advantage to be going into combat with such an experienced outfit, which had already proved to be one of the most effective B-26 groups in the ETO. The 391st was commanded by Colonel Gerald Williams, an able and dedicated leader who had trained at West Point. As one aspect of his leadership, he often flew the lead plane on his group's combat missions. So he asked nothing of us that he didn't do well himself, for which he was greatly respected. In private, however, he was often referred to as "Bull" Williams, a wry reference to his aggressive nature.

Chapter 7
Early Marauder Operations in North Africa and Europe

As Marauders had been phased out of the Pacific War, they had been phased into the war with Hitler and Mussolini. Operation TORCH, the invasion of North Africa that began with landings on November 8, 1942, was supported by B-26s, mainly as part of the Twelfth Air Force under the command of General James Doolittle. Operating against targets on both land and sea, usually at low altitude, their attacks on ships supplying enemy forces in North Africa were especially effective. But low-level attacks against strongly defended land targets were costly. Realizing that these heavy losses could not be sustained, General Doolittle ordered that land targets be attacked only from altitudes of about ten thousand feet, using a Norden bombsight in the lead aircraft of each formation. This important decision laid the basis for the subsequent success of B-26s in both the Mediterranean and European theaters.

Following the surrender of remaining Axis forces in North Africa on May 12, 1943, Marauders supported the invasion and capture of Mediterranean islands on the way to Italy, followed by the invasion of Italy itself and the heavy fighting as Allied troops moved northward toward Germany. In crossing the Mediterranean the first "stepping-stone" was the Italian island of Pantelleria, only thirty-two square miles in area but on the direct route from Tunisia to Sicily and too well fortified to bypass. B-26s contributed heavily to intensive attacks by aerial forces on the island's defenses, harbor, and airfield during late May and early June. The Italian garrison finally gave up on June 11 before any ground troops landed, the first time in history that surrender resulted from aerial assault alone.

In the ETO the Eighth Air Force, commanded by General Ira Eaker, initially included all American aerial combat units operating from England. The first B-26 group to arrive flew its initial mission on May 14, 1943, a low-level attack on an electricity generating plant at Ijmuiden, Holland. The bombs had fuses with thirty-minute delays to allow Dutch workers time to escape, but this also gave the Germans time to defuse the bombs. Three days later the Marauders tried again with twelve planes, one of which returned to base with an electrical failure. This time the Germans were waiting with intense flak, which destroyed five planes, and German fighters shot down the other six. General Doolittle's advice had been ignored and eleven crews had paid the price, one of the most complete disasters in the history of aerial combat. However, the lesson had finally been learned.

Following the Ijmuiden disaster, B-26 operations were suspended for two months to decide how to respond. Once again, consideration was given to dropping B-26 operations entirely, although the disaster resulted from poor policy rather than anything to do with the aircraft. Fortunately, it was decided to follow General Doolittle's tactic, which had proved so effective in the Mediterranean Theater. Marauders would again be used, but at medium altitudes with fighter escort, primarily in preparation for Operation OVERLORD, the Allied invasion of France planned for mid-1944.

Equally or more important, in October 1943 the Ninth Air Force, after serving in North Africa, was re-formed in England under the command of General Lewis Brereton. The Eighth Air Force retained responsibility for strategic bombing with heavy bombers, while the Ninth Air Force took over tactical operations with medium bombers and fighter planes. General Samuel Anderson, who had visited for several weeks with the 22d Bombardment Group in Australia, where he acquired great respect for the B-26, was placed in charge of the IX Bomber Command (later redesignated the 9th Bombardment Division). By April 1944 this unit included eight B-26 groups and three other groups using A-20 Havocs.

Strategic bombing concentrated on relatively large industrial and military targets deep within Germany that could be damaged or destroyed by large formations bombing from altitudes at or above twenty-thousand feet. By contrast, our tactical bombing from medium altitudes of ten thousand to fourteen thousand feet was usually in direct support of our advancing ground troops. We thus focused upon critical small targets requiring greater accuracy, hence the lower bombing altitude and smaller bombing formations. In brief, our operations were intermediate between those of heavy bombers in large formations at high altitudes, and dive-bombers acting singly at very low altitudes. So our designation as "medium" bombers was appropriate, since we were medium in size of plane, size of formation, and bombing altitude.

Prior to D-Day, our group's targets included enemy airfields, submarine pens, coastal defenses, marshalling yards, railroad and highway bridges, rocket sites, gun emplacements, and troop concentrations. The primary aim of the 391st, in common with other B-26 groups at that time, was maximum disruption of communications and supply lines to prepare for the invasion on D-Day. The success of that effort is documented by a report from Field Marshal Gerd von Rundstedt, German commander-in-chief in the West, to the German High Command: "In spite of the fact that the railway network is highly developed in the west and that innumerable highways and secondary roads exist, the enemy has succeeded, by concentrated and ceaseless attacks from the air, in disorganizing our supply [sufficiently] to cause such losses in railway stock and vehicles that supply has become a serious problem." This document, captured after D-Day, also indicated that trains could not get closer to the front than 94 to 125 miles, nor could they run on schedule.

During the early morning hours of June 6, 1944, a message from General Anderson was read to all medium-bomber crews at briefing, stating in part: "General Eisenhower, the Supreme Allied Command, last week charged me personally with informing you that he and all commanders of ground troops are deeply grateful for what you have done and are fully aware that *you have made possible the decision to land on the Continent*. The words which would express my own pride in your accomplishments do not exist." [italics added]

Shortly thereafter, responding to orders from General Eisenhower, all eight groups of Marauders lifted off to spearhead the D-Day invasion, leading the stream of Allied aircraft to bomb defense installations at the Normandy beaches only minutes before troops began landing. Until the beachheads were secured, the B-26s continued to bomb coastal defenses and enemy concentrations. Rail and road supply lines also were attacked, to prevent enemy reinforcements from reaching the beachheads, and fuel and ammunition dumps were bombed.

The landing at Utah beach received especially important support from B-26s, as described by John Dinou in *Flight Journal*, an aviation magazine. The B-26 armada of 424 planes was made up from eight different bomb groups. Leadership of this armada was assigned to the 344th Bombardment Group, in which the lead plane was piloted by Major Jens A. Norgaard, with Lieutenant Colonel Robert W. Witty, his copilot, acting as Command Pilot of the 344th. Of some interest, especially to myself, Colonel Witty is also a Quaker who became a Marauder man. A journalist both before and after the war, his own account of D-day was written in 1997 for the Tryon Daily Bulletin, a North Carolina newspaper.

The 344th formation consisted of 54 planes, formed into three boxes of 18 each. The weather was severe, with cloud cover extending from 5,000 feet up to almost 12,000. So the formation had to ascend through the clouds, under conditions of darkness, using running lights to prevent midair collisions. They then crossed the channel at somewhat above 12,000 feet. Effective bombing of D-day targets could only be accomplished visually, using the Norden bombsight, so prior to reaching Utah Beach they descended to slightly below 5,000 feet, far below their usual bombing altitudes. Their targets at Utah were three massive batteries of coastal guns embedded in concrete, each to be attacked by a box of planes, and all three aiming points were reached within 20 seconds of the assigned target times.

In his D-Day diary, General Brereton wrote that "...six medium groups of Marauders attacked seven pinpoint locations on Utah Beach and five coastal battery positions. Reports from the ground commander stated that the pinpoint bombing of the beaches was excellent and he later transmitted a commendation to bomber command." Reconnaissance P-38s reported destruction of all three coastal gun emplacements attacked by the 344th. This must have helped greatly by protecting Allied ships carrying troops to the beach. In addition, pillboxes and machine gun positions were bombed, while on the exposed beach itself, bombs destroyed land mines and made craters that offered protection for the landing troops. The last group of B-26s to hit Utah Beach, the 386th, completed dropping its bombs at 0625, only five minutes before the first wave of men hit the beach. Thus the defending Germans had almost no time to react between the cessation of bombing and arrival of the Allied infantry. As a result of all these effects, losses among the troops landing at Utah were quite low. And later on D-Day, the BBC reported that among all eight Marauder groups, "Only two planes were missing of the 400 [sent to strike] the German fortifications."

In summary, this must surely be ranked as one of the most successful and important bombing attacks in the history of air power.

D-Day also provided a rare instance in which the results of heavy bombers and B-26s could be compared, with similar targets and weather conditions. By contrast with the B-26s at Utah, the air support at Omaha Beach was ineffective and almost 3,000 men were reported lost or injured. Dinou says that 1,083 B-17s and B-24s dropped 2,944 tons of bombs through thick clouds and that all these bombs were reported officially to have landed about three miles inland from Omaha. Of course the fault lay not with the aircrews but in the folly of attempting, at that time, to bomb tactical targets blindly from above thick clouds.

As Allied ground troops began moving across Europe, Marauder targets moved ahead of them. These targets were usually supply lines bombed in preparation for further advances, rail and road bridges being destroyed with pinpoint accuracy, plus railroad roundhouses and marshalling yards, airfields, and troop concentrations. This pattern of operations was well established when our crew joined the 391st Bombardment Group at Matching Green.

Chapter 8
England and the Death of Myers

At Matching Green we first had to become accustomed to the V-1s, Hitler's buzz bombs, which passed overhead on the way to London. I never saw one but heard many at night. They were not true rockets, instead having pulse jet engines operating on liquid fuel. That type of jet engine was simple, cheap, and effective, but never became used in manned aircraft because it consumed excessive fuel and was intolerably noisy. Even from the ground, it sounded something like a Model T Ford, a sound well remembered from my childhood.

We were told there was no reason for concern while we could hear them. However, when the engine stopped, a V-1 could no longer remain airborne and immediately came down, so it was advisable to take cover. Although they occasionally fell short of London, they were little more than a nuisance to us. But they carried a ton of high explosive in the nose, so they caused great damage and loss of life when they fell in a crowded area such as London. The production of V-1s, and their planned launching from coastal sites in France, Belgium, and the Netherlands, had been impeded by Operation CROSSBOW, a program of determined air attacks in which the 391st Bomb Group had participated. This operation was later estimated to have delayed the use of V-1s by three to six months. The first V-1 fell in England on June 13, 1944, and the attacks reached a maximum during July and August, then tapered off sharply in September as launching sites in France were overrun by Allied troops. The V-1s had little military significance, but in England they killed 6,139 people and seriously injured 17,239, comparable to casualties reported from some battles of that period.

I wondered at the time how the V-1s and later V-2s got their names. It turns out they were named by the Germans, and the famous V-2, for example, stood for *Vergeltungswaffe zwei,* meaning "vengeance weapon two."

My letter home on September 23 described a two-day pass Chapin and I had in London. We took a room at the Red Cross, had good meals at various places, and enjoyed ourselves immensely. We did lots of sightseeing, and I took many pictures. My letter said, "One morning we attached ourselves to an expert guide who walked us around all the old historic spots—telling us about them as we went. There was Buckingham Palace, St. James Palace, St. James Park, Green Park, Parliament Square, Big Ben, Westminster Abbey, and all the rest." My letter also said, "Enclosed is a bit of Scotch heather—called lavender by the English—which I got from some poor lady who was selling it on the street. No English street is really complete without such an old lady selling her 'sweet lavender.' And it certainly is sweet—it smells so now at least. I hope it carries well." Apparently it did because it was still in the letter when I opened it more than fifty years later.

We also saw things in London that couldn't be mentioned in letters home. Most notably, this being just after the peak period of V-1 attacks, extensive damage was quite apparent. What I remember best was places where a bomb had sheared off much of a building, leaving plumbing fixtures (including at least one bathtub) hanging by the attached pipes with no other support. These sights were terribly dreary and affecting, but they served to remind us how fortunate we were that our own country had thus far been spared that kind of destruction. I heard a few stories from airmen who even experienced V-1s falling nearby during their nights in London, something Ken and I happily missed.

Each new crew was customarily assigned a plane of its own, and ours was already a combat veteran. Her name, conferred by her previous crew, which had just gone home, was *The Ginnie Gee*. This name was written on the nose in large letters, and directly beneath was a drawing in adequate but smaller scale that presumably depicted a lady named Ginnie. If the picture was any indication, she was generously endowed, ideally proportioned, and provocatively posed, typical of wartime art.

A few months after the war, I met a girl named Virginia, and we have been together ever since. From the beginning I spelled her nickname "Ginnie," and she has always said I was the first person to spell it that way, everyone else before having spelled it "Ginny" or "Jinny." The spelling on our plane was surely in my mind, and that is probably how my Ginnie got the new spelling of her nickname.

I'm sure none of us thought we would ever learn the origin of our plane's name, but amazing things happen. Our copilot, Don Fry, started flying for American Airlines immediately after the war and stayed with them for thirty-four years. Initially a copilot, one day he was on a long flight with a pilot he hadn't met before. While becoming acquainted they were surprised to learn that they had both been in B-26s, then that both had been in the 391st Bomb Group and even its 572d squadron. Finally, the pilot turned out to be John Blute, who had been pilot of the first crew of *The Ginnie Gee*, and who had named the plane after his wife. I had wondered how the "Gee" became part of our plane's name, so I recently asked John about it. He said his wife's maiden name was Virginia Glancy, and he had used "Gee" as a phonetic spelling of the first letter of her maiden name. So our plane's name was finally explained, and we ended up with two Virginias in its crews' families. Appropriately, *The Ginnie Gee* was a B-26G, the most refined and highly developed model.

One of my pictures of this plane, taken long after we became her crew, shows 130 bombs on the nose. So she had already flown that many missions, twice the tour of duty for any member of her crew. By the end of the war I had flown 43 missions, and though most were not in *The Ginnie Gee*, she remained in service during that time. So she became one of the longest-lived veteran planes of our bomb group with a probable total of about 150 missions.

Standard practice required each member of a new crew to fly his first mission with an experienced crew. For one of us, this first mission proved tragic. In September 1944 our ground forces had reached Germany, and flights to and from our targets were becoming excessively long. To keep pace with the advance, we were to move forward on October 1 to an airfield at Roye/Ami, almost fifty miles north of Paris. In preparation for that move, a ferry mission was undertaken on September 24 to transfer needed supplies to the new airfield. Though not a combat mission, it was treated as such for purposes of indoctrinating new crew members. Corporal John Myers, our radioman, whose workstation was directly to the left of my navigation station, was in one of the six planes.

The flight to Roye/Ami was uneventful, but the return flight was over a steadily developing cloud bank that covered England from ground level to a considerable height. Thus the letdown was extremely hazardous, with great danger of not seeing the ground until too late to level off. Fires were lit by ground crews to aid the returning planes, some of which landed safely. But three planes ran out of fuel and crashed, with the loss of all eleven crewmen on board, including Myers. Compounding this tragedy, some of the men killed had completed their sixty-five combat missions and were awaiting orders to return to the United States.

John Myers was buried with full military honors at the Madingley Military Cemetery near Cambridge, with all the rest of our crew in attendance. While mourning Myers, I found it impossible to avoid thinking what this might portend for the rest of us. Ever since I sighted a submarine that was almost certainly a German U-boat, the war had become steadily more personally threatening. Now this, the death of a crew member on his first mission, was a stark reminder of what could happen. So John's death was a sobering experience and seemed an inauspicious omen at the very beginning of our tour of missions.

As my own first mission approached, thoughts of it were seldom far from my mind. The weather was so bad that no one could know in advance on what day, or even what week, his first mission would occur. So it was something of a "sweat job," an apt and popular term at that time for stressful conditions. Of course, I knew that anyone could die at any time and that civilian life had many dangers of its own. But to face the real and imminent possibility of being violently killed or maimed for life was a new experience. Our daily routine provided some distraction, but not much, because all of our lives were "on hold" while waiting for the weather to clear. I don't recall feeling morbid or brooding about the possibilities, nor was I aware of such reactions in others. In fact, it is probably very rare that a person actually expects to be killed or wounded in wartime, being shielded from such serious apprehensions by the natural optimism of youth. Nevertheless, I felt in a state of suspended animation, and there was strong concern for what might happen, intermixed with the undeniable thrill of approaching an exciting new phase of my life.

On September 29, five days after the death of Myers, my first mission was flown in the crew of a pilot named Brockway. The purpose of this mission was to attack dragon-tooth defenses in the Siegfried Line at Webenheim, Germany. Since we were not a lead crew, my duties were minimal. As bombardier, I was needed only to toggle our bombs when the first bombs exited the bomb bay of the lead plane. As navigator, I had to keep continuous track of our position, in the event we became separated from our flight and had to return to base alone. Weather intervened, however, being so severe that we were unable to bomb visually, and the target was too small to bomb with GEE. We thus returned to base with our bomb loads intact, having encountered no flak or fighters. So my first mission was anticlimactic, indeed a "milk run." And it proved to be the only mission I flew from England.

Several years after the war, I ran into Brockway again in an amusing way. I was visiting friends in medical school at the University of Rochester, and an afternoon picnic had been planned with some of their fellow students. While driving to the picnic, the conversation turned to what nicknames we had been given, and someone asked if I had ever been called "Brownie." I said that strangely I had never been called that. A few minutes later we reached the parking site for the picnic, and while stepping out of the car I recognized Brockway getting out of a nearby car. He looked over at the same time, recognized me, and shouted, "Brownie!" Only then did I recall that Brockway was the one person who had ever called me Brownie, and he had called me that consistently. In all of the years since the war, this is the only time I have seen Brockway. And yet, out of all that time, he showed up at precisely the right moment to prove me mistaken. Of course, no matter how infinitesimal the likelihood, no coincidence is impossible. Even so, this one was hard to believe.

Chapter 9
On to France

As scheduled, on October 1, 1944, the 391st Bomb Group completed its move to Roye/Ami. This put us much closer to the front, thereby shortening our missions. It also left behind the English weather, but the winter weather over France and Germany proved little if any better.

Roye/Ami and its facilities had been occupied by the Luftwaffe since the fall of France in June 1940, and they had left only a few weeks before. The entire complex had been thoroughly bombed by Allied aircraft during the recent battle for France. In addition, the Germans had followed a scorched earth policy before retreating toward the Siegfried Line. The runways had been thoroughly bombed, all the wells in the area had been poisoned, and every building had been destroyed or severely damaged except for the German hospital, which was among nearby fields of sugar beets and well separated from all the other buildings. This hospital had been left intact with the German wounded still inside to be cared for by the advancing American forces.

Before our arrival the wounded Germans had been evacuated and the runways had been restored to usable condition, but little else had been done. So the place was a real mess, and the abandoned hospital was the only desirable building available for use as a barracks. The 391st Bombardment Group consisted of four squadrons, and all four squadron commanders were intent upon having the hospital for their aircrew officers. So Colonel Williams dealt out five-card poker hands. The 572d Squadron was represented by our operations officer, Major Joe Earll, who was well known for his success at poker. Fortunately, his luck held on this occasion and he won the hospital with a cold poker hand.

Other sections of our squadron were not so fortunate, having to repair their buildings or even live in tents. Even our building was entirely bare, with no furniture, heat, electricity, or water supply. We had flown in with only our personal effects. So our first task was to make our quarters more livable, especially warmer, because the weather was already cold.

Initially we had no bedding, so we slept on the floor in sleeping bags. Within a few days we had scrounged some burlap bags and dirty straw, with which we contrived crude mattresses. Meanwhile, several members of our group were using the squadron jeep to range the countryside for supplies, and they found an abandoned German warehouse with knock-down metal beds. We assembled enough of these to make double-decker beds for all of us, and some other bedding supplies were obtained. By October 9 my letter home reported finding a set of new but bare coil-type mattress springs, which I wrapped with heavy canvas and placed upon the flat springs of the metal cot. By then we also had some clean straw, which I used to fill a mattress cover. This made a comfortable mattress, topped off with a pillow brought from England. I don't think any of us had sheets, but we had blankets and sleeping bags that served well. My own bed proved one of the most envied in our squadron. So when we moved forward again in the spring, I left the bedframe but took everything else along in the bomb bay.

For the first few months, I was assigned to an eight-man room, which by October 9 was already complete with pinups. The atmosphere was sometimes noisy and garrulous, due mainly to a single individual, but there was also much conviviality. Fortunately, someone found a potbellied stove that was so new we had to burn off the varnish. Thereafter, cutting wood became one of our best and most productive exercises during the frequent periods of bad weather that prevented flying.

I can't recall what sanitary arrangements we used at first, which is probably just as well. In any event, by October 5 my letter home said,

"Yesterday saw the construction of what we proudly proclaim the most modern four-hole backhouse in this theater of operations. It's built over a bomb crater and is sheltered on all except the leeward side. We even have a tile walk leading out to it." The privilege of "test flying" this facility was claimed by our charismatic squadron commander, Lieutenant Colonel Floyd Miller, who reported it functioned perfectly in spite of not being airworthy.

At first we had so little water I remarked, in a letter on October 6, that the day before I had finally obtained two things, both much needed. One was a bath of sorts and the other was a haircut. The letter says, "I took my bath from a GI helmet with the aid of some soap and a washcloth. It's sheer flattery to call the process a bath, but such as it was it served the purpose." The haircut was equally rough but serviceable. It was obtained from a sergeant who claimed to be qualified, for twenty-five francs (about fifty cents) and a lightbulb, an item in very short supply.

Since no usable water was available locally, it was brought in from a source about eight miles away, using a water tank towed by a truck. Our building also lacked plumbing, but a pipe was soon installed that led water into a room with something like a horse trough that provided water for most of our needs. However, the greatest coup of all was provided by Eddie Mansfield, a bombardier, who somehow obtained a water heater that generated, in addition to hot showers, much appreciation for Eddie. Most surprising, perhaps, was the person who planned and performed the plumbing. Again, it was none other than Lieutenant Colonel Miller, who had been a bush pilot and a plumber in civilian life. In what other army in the world would someone, after rising to such a high rank, perform plumbing for the comfort of his junior officers?

The only drawback of our quarters was isolation from everything else in the squadron, which was located more centrally, as was the group headquarters where we were briefed and sent out on missions. The road from our quarters to everything else ran parallel with the runway, and it was some distance to facilities such as the mess hall, which was located in a former horse barn. We walked to our meals, which was good exercise, but were transported by trucks when going on missions. The biggest single inconvenience was making it to breakfast by 7:30, and later we even got around that. The abandoned hospital had a kitchen area, for which we obtained some basic kitchen equipment. Then two teenage French boys were found who became our breakfast cooks. I never understood the exact arrangement, but they seemed happy with it, probably because of the food and opportunities for barter. We also bartered with nearby farmers for eggs and other breakfast foods. Cigarettes were issued to all of us, whether we smoked or not; these were especially useful in barter, so nonsmokers such as myself fared well. At breakfast our eggs were cooked to order, and the kitchen was open until about 10:00, thus accommodating late risers who would be going on an afternoon mission.

With diligent scrounging and hard work, our quarters and living conditions thus became quite comfortable, and just in time for the onset of winter. In fact, considering the problems, our living conditions were so comfortable they certainly vindicated my choice of the Army Air Forces when "volunteering" for officer training.

Within walking distance was the village of Ami. It consisted of only about fifteen homes and followed the typical European plan that goes back to medieval times. All the local farmers lived there and went out to work their fields, some of which were the fields of sugar beets surrounding our barracks. So the village was a community of farmers with very little aside from their homes. Indeed, the only place of business was a primitive kind of tavern. Initially I went to the tavern a few times in the evenings, but there was hardly anyone to meet and talk with except ourselves, and that was better done in the barracks. Besides, we were well supplied with alcoholic beverages without going to a tavern. This resulted largely from the efforts of one of our pilots, Paul Young.

Paul had discovered an abandoned German warehouse and worked his way down into the basement until finally coming to a locked door. When this was broken open, he found himself in a storage cellar for the Wehrmacht's private stock. They must have left in a great hurry because there was no sign that they had tried to clear any of it out. It must have been quite a sight, something like a drinking man's concept of paradise. It was rather a pity in a way, because Paul didn't drink— but almost everyone else did, usually but not always in moderation.

Paul's find almost certainly supplied the potables that were distributed in a "seven-bottle deal." In this arrangement, selected bottles of liberated beverages were sold to any officer in the squadron for seven dollars. No one seemed concerned about who got the money, probably on the theory of not looking a gift horse in the mouth. I'm sure it wasn't Paul Young, so this is still an interesting and unanswered question. I can't remember the entire selection, but there was one bottle each of champagne, Spanish brandy, Armagnac, and scotch. Everything had been carefully selected by the Wehrmacht, and in most cases the vintages were from some time ago. For example, the champagne was a Charles Ducoin Brut, *Cuvée Speciale,* Extra 1933. And each bottle was stamped with a red label saying "Réservé à la Wehrmacht." I know this because I didn't open the champagne until back at home on the evening victory was declared over Japan (V-J Day), after which I made the bottle into a lamp that is now on my desk.

Though the town of Roye was much larger than Ami, and must have been fairly close, I don't remember going there for recreation or knowing of anyone else who did. So our life at Roye/Ami was quite isolated during the six-and-a-half months we spent there, which included the entire winter of 1944–45. The bad weather often gave us long periods of spare time, which in my case was spent mainly in reading and playing cards, primarily hearts, blackjack, and, of course, poker. Later, we received occasional 3-day passes to Paris, and even later there were rest leaves to Cannes on the French Riviera. But those pleasures were distant and very uncertain when we arrived at Roye/Ami.

Chapter 10
The Anatomy of a Combat Mission

T he four squadrons of the 391st Bomb Group were numbered 572d through 575th, and each squadron was a self-contained unit with its own planes, maintenance personnel, aircrews, barracks, and mess hall. In fact, all the living arrangements were so separate that I don't recall knowing anyone in our other three squadrons unless I had met him before joining the 391st. However, two or more squadrons usually were drawn upon to make up a mission.

When flying in formation our basic unit was called a "flight." It consisted of six planes, located as shown below and numbered by the convention we used to identify each position.

1

3   2

4

6   5

The first three planes, forming an inverted V, were called an "element." Thus a flight consisted of two elements flying one behind the other. The only named positions were the flight leader (1) and the "slot" position (4). Planes of the second element normally flew slightly lower than the first element to have a clear view of the planes ahead.

Three such flights joined together to form a "box," in which the lead flight was slightly ahead of the flights on its left and right. The flight on the left flew somewhat higher than the lead flight and was known as the "high flight," whereas the flight on the right was called the "low flight" because of being a little lower than the lead flight. Finally, two boxes usually flew one behind the other to complete the formation. So our formation normally contained thirty-six planes, but the number of flights varied between missions, depending upon the type of target and the number of separate targets to be attacked. In the rare cases when a mission consisted of three complete boxes, a "high box" flew to the left and behind the lead box, while the "low box" was on the other side of the formation.

At briefing, a "taxi sheet" (see p. 84) was posted on the bulletin board. This provided the entire layout of a given mission, with each plane identified by its first pilot. It also gave the order in which planes taxied out for takeoff, which was essential to assembling the formation in the air. Within each flight, planes took off in the order of their assigned numbers, as illustrated. Similarly, the flights took off according to their positions in the formation, following the same convention as for individual planes in a flight. Thus, planes streamed into the air in a logical sequence for the formation to be assembled quickly and efficiently, one flight at a time, with each flight moving into its assigned position behind the others.

Regardless of its size, the entire formation stayed together until reaching the initial point (IP) of the bomb run. This avoided many practical problems and provided excellent defense against fighter attacks, because the combined firepower of a tight formation of B-26s was formidable. At the target we usually bombed by single flights of six planes each. This was because many of our targets, such as bridges, were small enough to be effectively destroyed by the bombs from a single flight in tight formation. With bombing by flights, and our normal formation of six flights, we thus had six chances to destroy the target. For small targets, all flights assigned to a given target were instructed to attack that target. The target was occasionally destroyed by one or more of the early flights to attack. But our altitude of about two miles, combined with the clouds of dust and debris from the early bomb bursts, usually made it impossible to determine the effectiveness of the initial attacks. When bombing larger targets—for example, airfields—sometimes each box bombed as a unit or, more rarely, the entire formation bombed at the same time.

1st Box

Miller
8 637-A

Baehr
17 634-Q

Hanlon
13 719-F

Dickinson
1 972-S

Walker
23 747-T

Reynolds
1 000-L

Jobe
6 5811-G

Schleicher
15 947-U

Crim
16 797-P

Jacobs
15 799-T

McCarty
14 836-N

Alexander
2 252-Z

Whitson
17 895-T

Barker
2 028Y

Blute
10 809-0

Danforth
45 853-X

Koehl
46 620-B

Holliday
39 046-P

2nd Box

Brandon
37 373-U

Lowe
1-7808-X

Burridge
32 927-N

Newcomer
36 815-N

Matelsky
4 964-G

Evans
31 730-0

Shaffner
24 828-L

Bird
7 618-L

Cassiday
26 7841-A

Baxter
22 978-Q

Stanfield
30 720-K

Watkinson
29 818-L

Logan
47 7811-V

Salmon
30 248-V

Dearing
21 802-P

Bollinger
41 615-A

Garwick
29 841-S

Callison
31 851-M

Majka
34 865-D

Taxi sheet for a mission by the 391st Bombardment Group on June 8, 1944. The target was Valogne, near Cherbourg, France. (USAAF via Hugh Walker)

Prior to each mission, ground crew specialists fused and loaded our bombs. Most of the bombs were designed for demolition, varying in size from 100 to 2,000 pounds. While the smallest were used against airfields, the largest were used for very strong structures such as major bridges. On a few missions, however, we carried fragmentation bombs to attack troop concentrations. The surface of this type of bomb was deeply scored, like that of a hand grenade. Upon exploding, the outer casing thus fragmented into a great many deadly missiles.

A fuse to assure detonation was screwed into either the nose or the tail of each bomb. Inside the fuse was a plunger, which slid forward by inertia when the bomb struck something at the end of its fall. In standard fuses, this plunger struck and exploded a sensitive small primer charge, which in turn exploded the main charge of the bomb.

There also was a special type of fuse, with which an enemy airfield could be deactivated for at least two days. This fuse contained a small compartment filled with acid. When the bomb struck the ground, the plunger of this type of fuse broke open the pocket of acid, which then ate through a barrier to explode the primer charge. The time required for the acid to leak through the barrier could be preset, so that the bomb would explode almost immediately or up to two days after being dropped. The preset times were varied randomly among bombs, so a bomb fused in this way might explode at any time and was extremely dangerous to carry away. Also, prior to screwing the fuse into the bomb, a small lead ball was placed into a groove in the threads of the fuse. While the fuse was being turned clockwise during insertion, the ball could only move into a deepening part of the groove. If the fuse was unscrewed, however, the lead ball would be jammed into the shallowest part of the groove, which would explode the bomb instantly.

Our bombs were carried in racks on either side of the bomb bay. Before loading a plane with bombs, a wire was inserted through each fuse to lock the plungers and safety the bombs. After loading a bomb into the plane, this safety wire remained in the fuse, and its other end was attached to the bomb rack. When the bombs were released, the safety wires thus remained behind, and the bombs became armed as they left the plane.

The lead crew of each flight included an especially skillful bombardier and a separate navigator; hence the lead crew of a flight consisted of seven members instead of the usual six. The lead navigator of each flight provided navigation for his flight whenever it was separate from the formation. This was especially important when flights bombed independently and became so separated from the formation that each flight returned to base on its own. When the formation operated by boxes, the lead plane of each box did the navigation for that box, using two navigators. While one did conventional navigation, the other did GEE navigation and also GEE bomb aiming if required. Thus any plane leading a box carried a crew of eight. When the entire formation was together, the lead plane of the first box (the mission leader) performed the navigation for the entire formation.

Similarly, when bombing by flights, each lead bombardier performed the bomb aiming for his own flight, and when his first bombs left the bomb bay the other five bombardiers immediately triggered release of their bombs. The reaction times of the other five bombardiers always caused a slight delay, so the bombs from the following planes always impacted slightly ahead of those from the lead plane. Hence, the aiming point was normally chosen just short of the target; if the aiming was perfect, the flight's bombs would then impact from the aiming point forward to blanket the target. If bombing was by boxes, the lead plane of each box provided the aiming for its box, and more rarely the lead plane for the mission did the bomb aiming for the entire formation.

After "Bombs away!" each bombardier was expected to assess visually the accuracy and effectiveness of the results. This was done more reliably, whenever possible, by "strike photos." For this purpose, a camera was installed in both the lead plane and the slot plane of each flight. In each of these planes, the first bomb to drop was attached to the start switch of an intervalometer, which thus began running when the bomb left the plane. After a twenty-second delay, which prevented pictures from being wasted during most of the bomb's fall, the intervalometer triggered the camera to start taking pictures. This was done at one frame per second for thirty seconds, which covered well beyond the time when the bombs would reach the ground. This gave adequate time to assess the effects of the bombs, including any secondary explosions that might occur. The one frame/second was chosen to give useful sequential information. For example, sometimes one frame would show when a bomb was just entering a building, while the next frame would show the resulting explosion. Both kinds of information were helpful to photo interpreters at the 9th Bombardment Division, where the pictures were sent immediately after being developed and printed on a rush basis. The photo interpreters evaluated our results, as well as the types of bombs and fuses used to obtain them. Thus, their findings were often decisive in choosing our next target assignments and the bombing techniques to be used. In addition to strike photos, post-mission photos sometimes were obtained by a photo-reconnaissance squadron using lone but very fast P-38s that were modified and redesignated F-5s.

Airborne radar had become available at that time, and this was a great aid for both bombing and navigation in bad weather. Since it required specialized equipment and training, "pathfinder" squadrons provided this service. If it was known that weather would be bad over the target, and if the target was appropriate for bombing by the entire formation, a pathfinder would be assigned to our mission. It would then act as lead plane for the formation, providing both navigation and a radar bombardier. In still other cases, a separate pathfinder was assigned to each box.

Unfortunately, weather prediction was quite uncertain in those days, and the weather itself could change quickly, so we often had no warning that we would be unable to bomb visually. In such cases, the GEE system often provided a useful backup to the Norden bomb-sight, in addition to being helpful for navigation.

Our normal bombing altitude was about twelve thousand feet, much lower than that of heavy bombers. This lower altitude was necessary to hit pinpoint targets such as bridges, but it made flak similarly more accurate, so we were more vulnerable than heavy bombers to aimed, tracking flak. Although we were too high for light flak guns, which were usually 20mm or 37mm, the famous German 88mm gun could be used in many ways and was very accurate and effective against planes at our altitudes. We knew many of the fixed flak positions, which were plotted on our maps to facilitate navigating around them while flying to or from targets. However, mobile 88mm guns, either self-propelled or towed, could be turned upward and used with similar accuracy. Although rare, some fixed flak positions also had 105mm guns that were easily identified by the louder explosions and especially large, dense clouds of smoke.

When I reached the ETO, the Germans likewise had accurate radar-controlled flak. Thus, on several occasions, while flying over a solid undercast, flak found us and stayed with us as accurately as if we were visible. Barrage flak also was encountered sometimes over important and well-defended areas. This flak was timed for our altitude but not aimed at individual planes or flights, so in some ways it was less dangerous than aimed tracking flak, but when barrage flak was encountered it was concentrated in a small area.

The only way to evade barrage flak was by not flying over a heavily defended area. But some of our targets were defended by barrage flak, and in those cases the risk had to be taken. For tracking flak, the standard tactic was evasive action. It took some seconds for a flak battery to track us, and the flak shell required about twenty seconds to reach us from the ground. So changing our heading about every fifteen seconds was normally an effective tactic. But evasive maneuvering could not be used on a bomb run, for which the bombardier needed at least two minutes to achieve the requisite accuracy for pinpoint targets. Thus the bomb run was by far the most dangerous part of a mission.

If the flak was radar-controlled, we had another defense called "window," a tinsel-like material made from metal foil. A separate element of three B-26s, carrying window as well as bombs, flew about a thousand feet below and somewhat ahead of the bombing formation, an ideal position from which to spread a blanket of window beneath the bombers. Shortly after starting the bomb run, gunners tore open the packages of window and threw them out of the waist windows to disperse in the slipstreams. In theory the radar of the flak gunners would only detect the window, which would shield the planes above from radar view. Chapin noted on several occasions that all the flak bursts were in the layer of window, so the bombers above must have been effectively protected. The window planes were not protected, however, and may even have been targeted by canny flak gunners aiming at the growing point of the layer of window. Thus, the window planes literally "took the point," probably incurring extra risk to protect other planes in the formation. As with crews leading flights, the crew leading the window element contained both a lead bombardier and a lead navigator. Hence this element was prepared to bomb visually if weather permitted, or with GEE if the entire target area was obscured by clouds. The target assigned at briefing was often separate from the primary, but during the frequent bad weather, a target of opportunity was chosen if a suitable one was available for visual attack.

Of course, German fighters were extremely dangerous, but when I entered the war they were no longer a significant factor in day-to-day operations. That situation dated from shortly after the 391st went into combat on February 15, 1944. It undoubtedly resulted largely from "Big Week," which referred to the last week of February 1944, during which the Eighth Air Force made an intense and sustained attack upon the Luftwaffe with both heavy bombers and fighter planes. Nearly ten thousand tons of bombs were dropped, which destroyed or damaged more than seventy percent of the German war plants involved in aircraft production. In addition, more than six hundred German fighters were shot down, and almost a thousand German pilots and crewmen were killed or wounded.

In spite of the much-vaunted recuperative powers of German industry following bombing attacks, the Luftwaffe never recovered. In addition, German airfields were bombed intensively in preparation for D-Day, with special attention to hangars and exposed aircraft on the ground. The effectiveness of these operations was there for any airman to see by the conspicuous absence of the Luftwaffe on D-Day and its virtual disappearance thereafter from the skies over Western Europe. The only German planes I identified were occasional lone jets. Apparently, their remaining planes were being carefully hoarded, because during the Battle of the Bulge the Luftwaffe threw about sixty fighters against a single mission from our group.

In the event of being shot down in enemy territory but able to avoid initial capture, our final line of defense was an escape kit, an item of personal equipment that was issued to all members of aircrews. Everything was contained in a tight-lidded plastic box about an inch deep, five inches wide, and seven inches long. Instead of being flat, this box was curved around its long axis to better fit the calf pocket of our flying suits, where it was always carried during missions. The contents I recall included an escape map, miniature compass, morphine, matches, safety razor and blades, several kinds of paper money (French, Belgian, and Dutch), an identification card for travel in friendly countries, Benzedrine tablets for staying awake, halazone tablets for purifying water, and high-energy rations (such as chocolate).

In the case of one bombardier from our squadron, this escape kit saved his life in an unusual way. The parachute harness that bombardiers wore was attached to the body by three heavy straps. One was buckled across the chest, and the other two were buckled around the thighs at the groin. The parachute itself was a chest pack that was not worn all the time, which would have been cumbersome, but was snapped onto the harness just before bailing out. This man had been wearing his harness with the thigh straps buckled, but for some reason the chest strap was unbuckled. When he had to bail out, he grabbed his chute and snapped it on but forgot to buckle the harness across his chest.

When he pulled the rip cord he was upside down in the air, so the opening of the chute stripped the harness from his shoulders and almost stripped both leg straps from his legs. The only thing preventing this was the one leg strap becoming caught on the escape kit in its calf pocket. He thus ended up with only this tenuous connection between himself and the parachute as he descended upside down. He considered trying to reach up and grab the leg strap of the harness but didn't dare move for fear of dislodging the strap from the escape kit. So he descended like that all the way to the ground. When he saw the ground coming up to meet him, he tucked his head well down on his chest. Hitting on his shoulders, he broke a collarbone but was otherwise unhurt and was lucky enough to be back in friendly territory, where he received medical aid in good time.

In addition to enemy action, a very frequent danger was bad weather. Time after time, we flew missions when a dense cloud cover over our field extended upward many thousands of feet, sometimes all the way to our bombing altitude. Our standard operating procedure (SOP) called for oxygen to be available whenever we flew above ten thousand feet, where the atmosphere thins to only about half the oxygen content at sea level. But we were conditioned to our normal altitudes of up to fourteen thousand and didn't bother to carry oxygen. On one notable mission, however, we had to go all the way to eighteen thousand feet before finally breaking out of the clouds. Shortly after reaching our altitude for the flight to the target, it was SOP to put on our flak vests. These were made of nylon, into which overlapping manganese steel plates had been sewn, and a red rip cord was provided to separate the front and back sections for quick removal during an emergency bailout. Each vest weighed about thirty-one pounds, which was difficult enough to handle at our normal flying altitudes. At eighteen thousand feet, however, it was a memorable experience. By the time I had carried vests to Ken and Don, helped with putting them on, then returned to the navigator's position and put on my own, I was panting so hard I had to pant full time for quite a while before doing anything else. Amazingly, however, though the entire mission had to be flown at eighteen thousand feet to clear the clouds, this altitude caused no serious problem in any of the aircrews.

Whenever the cloud cover over our airfield was heavy, of course we had the problem of getting a formation of thirty-six or more planes safely up through it, then down again at the end of the mission. Nowadays it would be an air traffic controller's nightmare, and for good reason, but we did it routinely in the following manner. First, we formed up by boxes under the cloud cover and took up a heading for the target, with the two boxes well separated. Then, in each box the left and right flights turned forty-five degrees away from the lead flight and flew that heading for a timed interval, after which they turned back to the original heading. This put all flights on the original heading but safely separated, and in that manner we ascended through the clouds at a prescribed rate of ascent. After breaking out on top, we reassembled each box and then the complete formation. At least that was the theory. Sometimes a flight became separated from the formation and had to head for the rendezvous, a designated point of final assembly before proceeding into enemy territory.

Within a flight, we flew such tight formation that normally it was possible to get through the clouds without the flight itself breaking up. Indeed, it was considered safer to do it that way than to break up the flights and have individual planes all over the sky. Within a flight, each non-lead plane usually needed to keep visual contact with only one other plane. However, if visual contact with that plane were lost, as sometimes happened in exceptionally dense clouds, it was necessary to move immediately away from the flight to a safe distance before reassuming the original heading.

Upon return to base, our letdown through the clouds was similar to the ascent. In spite of the great many times our group went through this process, I never heard of an accident resulting from formation flying in heavy weather. This seems nothing less than a miracle, and pilots from those days still speak of it with awe. Surely our safety record in heavy weather was a strong testimonial to the procedures used, but equally or more to the skill and vigilance of a remarkable group of pilots.

Aviation Cadet Ken Brown. (USAAF)

The farm near Purcellville, Virginia, where I was raised. (Author's collection)

My mother with her beloved cows. (Author's collection)

An aircrew of the pioneering 22d Bombardment Group, operating from Queensland, Australia, in early 1942. The lack of uniforms of any kind suggests the primitive conditions under which they operated, and their cheerful demeanor in this picture is typical of the high morale that was somehow maintained. Note also the intriguing nose art on their B-26 and the eight bombs painted below the cockpit, indicating that the plane had already completed at least eight missions. (Pima Air & Space Museum Archives)

A B-26 of the 22d Bombardment Group undergoing maintenance work. To the right is a primitive crane for lifting heavy parts. Though of unknown origin, it appears typical of devices that had to be improvised on the spot. (Pima Air & Space Museum Archives)

Ken Chapin using his personality and binoculars to charm two Irish children. (Author's Collection)

The author biking in Northern Ireland. (Author's Collection)

With their 2,000-horsepower engines warmed up and turning over, B-26s of the 332d Bombardment Group awa their turns for takeoff from Andrew's Field, England, in September 1943. The 322d was the first B-26 group to begin operations from England against targets in the ETO. (USAAF)

An example of B-26 operations against enemy supply lines in preparation for D-Day. Hasselt, in eastern Belgium, contained a major rail junction that was attacked by 200 Marauders on April 10, 1944, with the illustrated results. The white smoke is an exploding ammunition train that left a crater 150 feet long and 40 feet wide. (USAAF)

The devastated rail junction at Hasselt with all of the main lines cut—one in seventeen places—by 1,000-pound bombs. (USAAF)

An example of what flak could do to a B-26. Over Toulon, France, on August 20, 1944, this airplane's right engine was completely blown away. This picture was taken only moments later, as the engine was falling with its propeller still turning. The right main landing gear has dropped and the wing tank has burst into flames. Only two crewmen got out.
(The photo was taken from a nearby plane by Staff Sergeant Peter J. Holmes.)

Among the first aircraft over the Normandy beaches on D-Day, all eight groups of B-26 Marauders attacked coastal defenses and enemy supply lines. Shown here are eight airplanes from the 386th Bombardment Group during their second or third D-Day mission. Like all B-26s that day, they wore invasion stripes to avoid being attacked by friendly forces. Though the aircrews probably had little time to enjoy it, this photo also shows their grandstand view of the sea crowded with ships, many of which appear to be heading for the beaches, during this momentous event in human history. (USAAF)

The Ginnie Gee after 70 missions, photographed with its new crew. Left to right: Ken Chapin, pilot; Don Fry, copilot; Ken Brown, bombardier-navigator; Don Fawcett, flight engineeer and tail gunner; Glen Hemund, radio operator and waist gunner (replacing John Myers); Bob Graves, armorer and top turret gunner. (USAAF)

Sporting bombs recording 130 missions, The Ginnie Gee with her efficient and loyal ground crew Left to right: Robert L. Sanders, crew chief; Rea, Mac, and "Pop." (USAAF)

A pair of 391st Bombardment Group B-26s in flight over France.
(Pima Air & Space Museum Archives)

The abandoned German hospital at Roye/Ami that became the barracks for aircrew officers of our 572d Squadron. (Author's collection)

Cutting and gathering wood to heat our barracks. Left to right: Ken Fagan, a bombardier friend who was killed by a direct hit to the nose of his plane while flying with Paul Young on February 24, 1945; Larry Chatellier, a pilot; Woodrow "Chuck" Fry, a pilot and the brother of Don Fry, the copilot in Ken Chapin's crew.
(Author's collection)

The skeleton of a burned-out hangar and an airplane of our bomb group at Roye/Ami, our new base north of Paris, to which we moved on October 1, 1944. Previously occupied by the Luftwaffe, almost everything at this base had been destroyed before the Germans retreated farther east. By December, when this photo was taken, snow was seriously impeding our operations. (Pima Air & Space Museum Archives)

A flight of six planes of the 391st Bombardment Group flying in formation over France.
(Pima Air & Space Museum Archives)

A B-26 with its nose protected by a canvas cover. The bombs nearby await loading for an upcoming mission. (Pima Air & Space Museum Archives)

Armorers loading a 2,000-pound bomb at Roye/Ami, December 1944. (Pima Air & Space Museum Archives)

View from inside the bomb bay while a bomb is being lifted by a winch. Attached to the bomb is a shackle that will be secured to the bomb rack when the bomb has been lifted to the appropriate level. The bomb racks on either side of the catwalk are slightly tilted to avoid any contact with bombs as they drop from the plane. Spare shackles are lying upon the catwalk. Although the catwalk was very narrow—only about six inches— it sometimes had to be traversed in flight with the bomb-bay doors open. Note also the narrow space between the left and right bomb racks, which made no allowance for a notably overweight crewmember, none of which I recall in B-26s. (USAAF)

Although the nose of a B-26 was covered mainly with Plexiglas, the oval section beneath the bombsight was made of flat optical glass to improve bombing accuracy by avoiding distortion of the bombardier's view through the bombsight. A small hinged window was also provided—to the right of the glass oval in this picture—that the bombardier could reach through to clean the outer surface of the glass. A pair of crewmen model the flack vests and helmets that were worn over enemy territory. (USAAF)

Captain William Smith, a bombardier with the 386th Bombardment Group, mans his Norden bombsight in the nose of a B-26. (USAAF)

A bombardier's view of his Norden bombsight. Note the soft rubber eyepiece, through which the ground was viewed, and the machine gun stowed to the left and above the bombsight. The photo was taken by W. Niezhalski, who apparently found the nose rather cramped, since his left foot is also in the picture.

The cockpit and instrument panel of a B-26. The PDI may be seen at the extreme left of the upper row of instruments. Siince bombing was the primary purpose of this aircraft, the PDI was placed directly in front of the pilot, the position of highest priority in designing the instrument panel. At the lower right corner of this picture, a portion of the tunnel leading into the nose can also be seen. (Glenn L. Martin Co.)

B-26s of the 391st Bombardment Group attack the marshalling yard at Hirson, France, on March 25, 1944. (Pima Air & Space Museum Archives)

Bombs falling from the first four planes of a flight of B-26s. Each plane is dropping eight 500-pound bombs. Bombs were released first from the lead plane, and the first two of these bombs are already out of sight below the picture. The other three bombardiers toggled release of their bombs upon seeing the first bomb appear from the lead plane. Apparently the trigger finger of the bombardier in the slot plane was a little slower than the trigger fingers of the other two bombardiers.

View of bombs dropping from the lead plane of a flight, as seen from the slot plane of the same flight.

Flak bursts around a B-26 as it releases its 500-pound bombs on an enemy installation in northern France on May 9, 1944. (USAAF)

The effect of an 88mm flak burst upon a 391st Bombardment Group B-26 on May 20, 1944. Although the rudder and left elevator were almost destroyed, this airplane was somehow flown back to Matching Green, England, where it was repaired and continued to fly for a total of 96 misisons.(USAAF)

Contrary to its early reputation, this B-26 is flying perfectly straight and level with one engiine out and its propeller feathered, just as The Ginnie Gee was flown by Ken Chapin when we were forced to abort and return from a mission. (USAAF)

Effects of the severe winter weather of 1944-45 upon B-26 operations from France. Here snow is being cleaned from airplanes, and runways also had to be cleared. This photo shows aircraft of the 386th Bombardment Group around Chirstmas 1944, when our B-26s were finally able to give crucial help during the Battle of the Bulge. (USAAF)

An American in Paris for the first time — the author under the Eiffel Tower.
(Author's collection)

B-26s flying a mission just above a solid undercast, as occurred so often while flying missions over Europe during the winter of 1944-45. (USAAF)

A strike photo from our mission to Konz-Karthaus, Germany, on December 24, 1944, the second day weather permitted us to fly during the Battle of the Bulge. Our primary target was a railway bridge over the Mosel River that was part of an important German supply line. Here, 1,000-pound bombs score direct hits on the bridge and nearby railway lines. (USAAF)

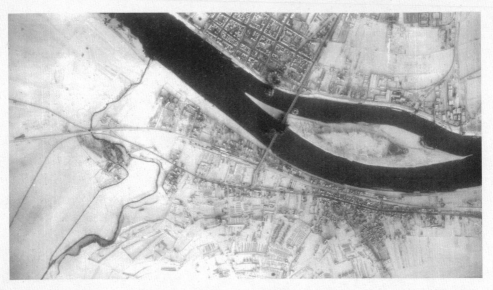

Strike photo of the Hermann Göring highway bridge over the Rhine at Neuwied, Germany, which we attacked with 2,000-pound bombs on January 16, 1945. I was still flying with Chapin's crew, and our flight was credited with direct hits. This photo may not show our bombs, but it records direct hits on one span, and later reconnaisance showed that both main spans were destroyed. (USAAF)

One of the early lead crews with which Wegenek and I flew. Standing, left to right: Dana Wetherbee, pilot; Ed Wegenek, bombardier; Ken Brown, navigator; Charlie Harrison, copilot. Kneeling, left to right: Staff sergeants William Kiefer, Robert Clark, and Gerald Gould, gunners. This photo was taken when Wetherbee's plane, Lady Belle, had flown 100 missions. Note Wegenek's Colt .45 in a shoulder holster, where he always carried it during missions. (USAAF)

A rail bridge at Bad Oeynhausen, Germany, which our group attacked on February 21, 1945, while Wegenek and I were flying with Wetherbee. This photo shows the bridge as it was blanketed with direct hits by 2,000-pound bombs from a flight of airplanes in our formation. The flight that did this great job is not identified. (USAAF)

Bonde's lead crew in front of an A-26 Invader. Left to right: Preben Bonde, pilot; Ken Brown, navigator; Naurbon Perry, gunner and flight engineer; Ed Wegenek, bombardier. (USAAF)

A marshalling yard in Kreuztal, Germany—one of the four targets attacked by our group during Operation CLARION on February 22, 1945. This strike photo shows direct hits by the 500-pound bombs from a flight of B-26s. (USAAF)

A flight of B-26s over a target in the Pas de Calais area during the battle for France. One airplane has been hit by flak that ignited fuel in the right wing tank, and the resulting flames are almost engulfing one of the trailing planes. This illustrates what happened in one of our flights on February 24, 1945, when the flight leader took a direct hit that ignited the fuel in a wing tank, and the resulting flames swept over the slot plane and burned off the fabric from the control surfaces on one side. (USAAF)

Our B-26 after Bonde crash-landed it at Roye/Ami with a collapsed nose wheel on February 24, 1945. Note the chewed off underside of the nose. (Photo by Duryea Warn, via Naurbon Perry)

Joe Grow's B-26 after he crash-landed it right behind us on February 24, 1945. His left main landing gear collapsed, followed by the other landing gears, so he ended up in a belly landing. Note especially the broken left wing, the severely bent propeller blades, and that one of his landing wheels broke off but came to rest beside the airplane. (USAAF via Joe Grow)

A Luftwaffe landing field at Babenhausen, Germany, is blanketed by more than a thousand 100-pound bombs on March 14, 1945. On this mission I was the GEE navigator for Captain Crumal, the mission leader. (USAAF)

A factory area at Dinslaken, Germany, is hit on March 23, 1945 by twenty-four 1,000-pound bombs aimed by Wegenek. On this mission I was the GEE navigator for Colonel Williams, who led the mission, and Wegenek was the bombardier for a separate flight.(USAAF)

A Douglas A-26 Invader, to which the 391st Bombardment Group had converted, at our new air base near Asch in eastern Belgium. (Pima Air & Space Museum Archives)

Our airfield at Asch, as seen from beneath the right wing of an A-26. Note the control tower for the airfield, the wind direction indicator (better known as a wind sock), the ever-present ambulance and the metal mesh that surfaced the airfield to prevent airplanes from sinking into the mud. (Pima Air & Space Museum Archives)

The delightful barracks at Asch that I shared with three other officers. (Author's collection)

In the lovely garden at the home in Zwartberg of Monsieur and Madame Hanot, who are wearing the uniform caps provided by me and a bombardier friend, Leroy Gresham, who is standing to the left. Other guests in this photo are relatives and friends of the Hanots. (Author's collection)

Lieutenant Colonel Joe Earll, operations officer and then commanding officer of our 572d Squadron. He is standing by an A-26 in May 1945, just before departing Asch after completing his tour of missions. (Pima Air & Space Museum Archives)

Major Manley Richmond, standing by an A-26 in May 1945, when he succeeded Joe Earll as commanding officer of the 572d Squadron. Inexplicably, he was killed on the way home when his A-26 went into a steep dive and plunged into the Mediterranean Sea. (Pima Air & Space Museum Archives)

Following our wedding, at a reception in Ginnie's family home. Standing, left to right: Ginnie's grandmother, mother, and father; my mother and father; my sister, Ruth, and her husband, Walter Kemp. Seated: the bride and groom, wedded at last.

Chapter 11
My First Missions from France

Incredibly, our group flew its first mission from Roye/Ami on October 2, the day after moving to our new base. But it was not a success, owing to weather. Throughout the entire month, weather restricted our operations so severely that the group flew only eight missions, of which our crew flew but two. This gave us time to get our base and quarters into reasonable condition, and these activities were good for morale. Otherwise, the inactivity would have been hard because everyone seemed anxious to get on with the war, knowing what the ground troops must be going through and how badly our help was needed.

My own first mission from France was also my first with Chapin's crew; it occurred on October 8, when we were sent to a heavily defended area near Breskens on the Dutch coast. The mission itself was not noteworthy, but it proved typical of many others during that period.

Like most morning missions, it began at about 5:00 A.M., when each man on alert for the mission was awakened by an orderly. Of course he used a flashlight, but the beam was kept shaded with his hand. In fact, the orderly didn't seem to like this part of his duty at all, because he was always considerate and even apologetic. After gently shaking each of us awake, and making sure we would stay awake, he crossed off each name on his wake-up list. This list must have been carefully compiled, and the orderly must have had an accurate map of who occupied each bed, because I don't recall ever being awakened by mistake.

We then dressed for the mission. Since this was usually done in complete darkness to avoid waking our bunkmates, we had to know just where each needed item was located. The weather in October was already cold, so I first pulled on long underwear, then the flying coveralls, which were made from a strong and warm material that was probably wool. My flight jacket for cold weather was sheepskin, but we used the famous leather A-2 jackets for more moderate weather. Some aircrew members also used sheepskin pants, but I did not. They were heavy and cumbersome and not necessary in the enclosed parts of the plane where I worked. The waist gunner, on the other hand, had to stand by the open waist doors and must have needed them badly. We also had sheepskin boots, which were worn over our shoes. The boots were clumsy for walking, so I tied the laces together and carried them until after boarding our plane. I also stuffed a pair of gloves into one of the many pockets of the coveralls. Military identification tags (our "dog tags") were not worn around the neck at all times. But we were careful never to forget them when preparing for a mission, because anyone shot down and captured without them would almost certainly have been executed as a spy. Needless to say, we were equally careful to secure the escape kit in a calf pocket of the coveralls. Thus girded, it was time for breakfast.

We could have walked, but it was probably thought wise to save our energies for the mission itself. So we were driven by trucks to the squadron mess hall, where all aircrew for the morning mission were treated to a hearty breakfast. Though I never heard it mentioned, I think we all knew it was a good idea to dig in, because the delay until another meal might be long indeed for anyone who was shot down.

After breakfast we were driven to the Operations Building, where senior officers of our bomb group briefed all aircrew officers assigned to the morning mission. We learned the makeup of the formation and the location of each plane within the formation. This was also written on a taxi sheet, which was posted on the bulletin board for ready reference before leaving the briefing room. Other subjects covered included location of the rendezvous point and IP, identity and nature of the target, expected weather, and anticipated enemy opposition such as flak batteries along our route. If a fighter escort was planned, we were also given the time and place where they were expected to join us.

Following this general briefing, bombardiers and navigators were given a special briefing covering some of the same matters in greater detail. Particular attention was given to factors that should be considered if weather precluded bombing the primary target. In such an event, the final choice of a secondary target was usually made by the lead navigator of each flight, based upon the relative priorities of alternate targets and the expected flak at each, as learned at briefing, and weather in the direction of alternate targets, as observed from the vicinity of the primary target. So this aspect of the briefing was quite important.

After briefing, a ten-to-fifteen-minute break was allowed for those wishing to meet with a minister, priest, or rabbi for a brief prayer service. As a Quaker, I believed that all men have equally direct access to God. Thus, I didn't participate in group prayers but may have said a private prayer—I just don't remember. All aircrews were then loaded into trucks and driven to the hardstands where the planes were parked.

By this time our plane had been fully checked out by its maintenance crew. Other ground crew specialists had fused our bombs and loaded them into racks on either side of the bomb bay. Extensive preflight checks also were carried out at this point by Ken and Don, in consultation with the crew chief. And all other aircrew members checked to see if everything they needed was available and in good working order, our gunners having begun this process while the officers were being briefed.

At Chapin's order we all boarded the plane, and I donned my flying helmet, the classic closely fitting leather type with a chin strap that was used by all crew members. Over each ear it contained a built-in earphone that was the receiving component of the intercom. The sending component was a separate "throat mike" consisting of two small microphones, one on either side of the larynx and held in place by a strap around the neck. Thus equipped, we could talk to each other without using our hands, except that each crew member had to depress a switch while speaking. Our helmet earphones and the throat mike had short cords, with which we could plug into the intercom system at any crew position. This was especially useful to a crew member like myself who worked in two different crew positions.

After starting and warming up the engines, we taxied to the runway, awaited our turn, and took off. We then joined the formation at our assigned location and climbed to the assigned altitude of the mission, at about twelve thousand feet. There we all put on flak vests. The pilots could not do this without help, so I took flak vests to Ken and Don and assisted with putting them on. Then I put on my own and prepared to move into the nose of the plane. The tunnel to the nose was directly in front of Don, who had to move his seat back as far as possible before I could enter the tunnel, which was so narrow I could barely crawl through it. Once in the plane's nose, I remained there until we neared our air base on the return flight.

During the mission I continually kept track of our position, using pilotage, dead reckoning, or a combination of the two. While still over France but nearing the target area, I was startled to see a smoke trail that suddenly went from the ground to a great height in just a few seconds. I estimated it to be at least fifty miles ahead—hence in enemy territory. The smoke trail went up almost vertically, so it had to be from something exceedingly powerful and fast. Then more of the trails appeared, at least half a dozen, all in the same general location and all looking much the same. Ken and Don also saw these smoke trails, and we discussed them over the intercom. The only explanation we could think of was German jet fighters, so Ken alerted the gunners to keep a close lookout. But our formation was not attacked.

Upon reaching the bomb line (the line beyond which there was no danger of bombing our own troops), the pilots put on "flak helmets," protective steel helmets like those used by American ground troops. Owing to insufficient headroom in our positions and/or difficulty in moving about within the plane, neither the gunners nor I could take full advantage of that extra protection. Our flight of six planes was the high flight on the left side of the first box, and we had been ordered to bomb by flights. The order of bombing by flights was flexible, but flights in a given box usually bombed in the order of lead flight, high flight, and low flight. When our flight reached the IP, the bombardier in the lead plane warned his pilot that their bomb bay doors were about to be opened. When the bombardier then opened the doors, the pilot immediately advanced his throttle to counteract the increased drag. Otherwise the lead plane might have slowed too quickly for the slot plane to avoid a crash. The bombardiers in the other five planes, including myself, watched the lead plane closely and opened our doors in unison as the lead plane's doors began to open.

As we approached the target, I kept my hand on the toggle switch for bomb release and intently watched the bomb bay of the lead plane. When the first bomb appeared, I flipped the switch as quickly as possible, then watched as the bombs from our flight fell toward earth. This was the first time I dropped bombs in combat, so it was exciting. But the results were disappointing because I observed no direct hits, and our results were officially rated as poor, probably because bad weather during that period made accurate bombing almost impossible. This was also the first mission when I saw flak; though it was in the target area, it was distant, scattered, and no threat to us or our plane.

Our return to base was uneventful. After landing and taxiing to our hardstand, we were picked up by trucks and conveyed to a room for debriefing. This was conducted by our squadron's intelligence officer, who always asked if we had observed anything unusual or of special interest. When I described the smoke trails, he said they must have been German V-2s, the first true rockets employed in wartime. So I first learned of these new weapons, ballistic missiles fueled with liquid oxygen, by seeing them launched. Like the V-1s, they carried a ton of high explosive, but they superseded the V-1s for terror bombing of London, mainly because of greater accuracy in hitting that city. In addition, the V-2s traveled at great height and came down at supersonic speed, so they gave no warning and no chance to take shelter. Although the first of these missiles had hit London on September 8, 1944, none of our crew had heard of them until we were informed by the intelligence officer, an indication of how little news we had been receiving.

As we left the building after debriefing, attending medics offered each man a generous amount of "medicinal bourbon." This had been found to relieve pent-up tensions and stress, so it had become routine after every mission. Though I felt no need of it at first, I always accepted it, and as the missions added up, so also did my appreciation for this thoughtful gesture.

The weather was little better in November, during which our bomb group flew twelve missions. We started to fly six of these, but had to abort and return from one of them on a single engine. This was a more noteworthy event in the B-26 than in other twin-engine aircraft, because the B-26's high wing loading provided little reserve lift for single-engine operation. We had completed joinup and were flying at about ten thousand feet, when Ken noticed oil streaming from the left engine. Instead of waiting for the engine to quit, he immediately shut it down, hoping to save the engine by averting the danger of fire when the oil ran out. He also "feathered" the engine's propeller by flipping a switch that oriented all four blades with their edges directed forward. This hastened stopping the engine, which took only about eight seconds, and also reduced drag from the dead engine. Our radioman was not using his compartment at the time, and I was sitting there looking out the left window, when the prop suddenly slowed and stopped before my eyes. If I hadn't seen the prop stop I wouldn't have known anything had happened, because Ken had readjusted so quickly and smoothly to the drastically altered requirements of single-engine flight that the plane never wavered.

I grabbed and donned my chest chute in case it would be needed, but it wasn't. We were fully loaded with bombs, which most pilots would have jettisoned in a field. But not Ken. Having grown up on a farm, he explained afterward that he didn't want to give some friendly French farmer the problem of bomb disposal. Fawcett, our flight engineer, also had seen the oil trail and rushed forward to the cockpit. As the plane lost altitude, he kept his hand near the salvo-release control in case the bombs would have to go for us to remain airborne. Becoming increasingly nervous, he asked several times if he should release the bombs. Ken always said "No," and we finally leveled off at about a thousand feet.

Upon reaching our airfield, Ken alerted the tower that he would come straight in, with no possibility of going around for a second try. Then he carefully lined up his approach to make full use of the runway, because its length of about a mile gave little reserve for emergency conditions. With its high landing speed, a B-26 was hard enough to stop under the best of conditions. In this case our pair of 2,000-pound bombs significantly increased both our speed at touchdown and the plane's inertia. Although Ken chopped the throttle of the right engine just after touchdown, the plane slowed very little for quite some time. When it finally slowed enough for braking to be effective, he braked gently at first to prevent losing control and ground looping. Then he braked harder, while using both brakes and rudder to steer a straight course. The plane was almost stopped as he neared the end of the runway, so he used its final momentum to turn into the last available taxi strip before coming to a stop. Looking around, he noticed a jeep racing toward the plane. It pulled up near the bad engine and our assistant group commander, a lieutenant colonel, stood up and shouted through his cupped hands, "Where are your bombs?" When Ken called back, "They're in the bomb bay," the colonel just shook his head in wonder, sat down, and drove away.

Soon thereafter, our ground crew arrived to tow the plane to its hardstand. The damaged engine had already served for almost 100 missions and had finally succumbed to metal fatigue, so it had to be replaced in spite of Ken's efforts to save it. This made extra work for the ground crew, but they didn't seem to mind, and their relief at having us back was touching. We knew that Sandy, our crew chief, thought of us as "his boys" and worked hard to keep us safe. I also learned later that another member of our ground crew always went into a nearby work shack, just after we departed on a mission, to pray for our safe return. With such fine men as those, we were lucky indeed to be "their boys."

As a side effect of so much weather flying during these early missions, I became acquainted with an optical phenomenon called the "pilot's cross." While flying in direct sunlight with a dense undercast just below, which we were doing much of the time, of course the sun casts a shadow of the plane on the clouds below. And something that looks like a rainbow forms a perfect circle around the shadow of the plane. Presumably it is called a pilot's cross because of being seen first by pilots, and because the shadow of the plane looks like a cross. In our case the phenomenon was usually under the plane and thus seldom seen by our pilots. But it was ideally observed by a bombardier in the Plexiglas nose, so I saw it often and found it strikingly beautiful. And I was astonished to note that although the shadow of a single plane was closely fitted by the circle, the shadow of a flight of six planes was closely fitted by a much larger circle, with no circles around shadows of the individual planes in the flight.

After the war I studied light and optics as background to my research in retinal physiology. I thus learned that a true rainbow is readily explained by the refraction of light in water droplets. I also learned that the pilot's cross is a special case of something called a glory, which has been known since ancient times. It may be seen when the sun is near the horizon and the shadow of an observer on a hilltop is cast upon a cloudbank in the valley beyond. Under those conditions, the glory is a rainbowlike circle around the shadow of the observer's head, and the name appears to come from mystical or religious interpretations.

Unlike the rainbow, the glory has stubbornly resisted physical explanation. A promising beginning was made in the early 1970s, and further progress followed, but an adequate explanation remains elusive. My observation that a glory can surround the shadow of an entire flight of planes, without appearing around the shadows of individual planes in the flight, does not appear to have been heretofore reported or taken into account. Needless to say, any complete theory must also explain this fact.

Chapter 12

Paris

My fifth mission was flown on November 10, and my first three-day pass to Paris began the next day. Since my early missions had been routine except for bad weather, I hadn't yet experienced any significant stress, so the timing of my first pass appeared unrelated to combat. Nonetheless, I had looked forward to it with great anticipation because of our isolation at Roye/Ami and the fascinating reputation of Paris.

We were taken in by trucks and disembarked at the American Express building, a major focal point for American troops entering or leaving Paris. As I climbed over the tailgate and jumped down to the street, someone I knew was getting out of another truck. He saw me at the same time and we started running toward each other, followed by much handshaking and backslapping, as if we were best friends. Then we stood back, looked at each other, and tried to sort out why we were acting like that. We couldn't remember each other's names or even where we had become acquainted. We had come to Paris from different airfields, and apparently we had both been living in isolated groups in bad weather for long enough that we were unconsciously desperate to meet someone from earlier times. This probably accounted for our instinctive reaction, and I felt rather abashed, as I believe he did. We exchanged names, which proved familiar, then tried to find out where we had known each other. After running a few times through the training bases each of us had attended, we finally remembered one that neither of us had mentioned. At the classification center in Nashville, Tennessee, we had bunked near each other. So we chatted a bit more and parted, amused and amazed, and we haven't met since. But I have always remembered this interesting result of the strangeness of our lives during that period.

Ken Chapin and I were together on this pass, during which our days were spent mainly in seeing famous sights and landmarks such as the Eiffel Tower. For two farm boys in Paris the first time, this was quite exciting. Shopping was also enjoyable because exotic items were available that were almost unobtainable elsewhere, such as perfumes that made ideal gifts to send home. We walked a great deal, but for long distances used the métro (subway), the only public transport available aside from a few taxis that never could be found. The métro must have been terribly crowded because one of my letters home said, "At one place it took three trains in a row to get four of us to the next station. One man got on each of the first two and Chapin and I both managed to get on the last."

The most memorable times, however, were the evenings enjoying the famous Parisian nightlife. We were billeted in the Lafayette Club, a hotel run by the Red Cross for servicemen on leave. The first night there, a group of us went out with some American Red Cross girls who were likewise on leave, in their case from front-line "clubmobiles" that served doughnuts, coffee, and brief moments of companionship—the latter no doubt most valued. We went to the Bal Tabarin, one of the most famous nightclubs. As noted in my letter home soon afterward, "It was really a beautiful place. There were two orchestras playing both French and American music, and we danced and danced and danced. It was wonderful just to talk to an American girl again and spend an evening dancing." Indeed, it must have been satisfying because Chapin and I spent the next evening at our hotel, "over innumerable cups of coffee and doughnuts, exchanging viewpoints of the war with two artillerymen."

During my second pass to Paris, December 5–7, the first night was almost too interesting. Along with a number of fellows I didn't know well, we went club-hopping. This time we shunned the famous ones and concentrated on some of the less famous (perhaps even a few infamous) ones. All of them had French girls who were easy to meet, and the reason was obvious. They were almost all selling something—either drinks for the mutual benefit of themselves and the club, or themselves in a much more private enterprise. Sometimes a Frenchman was also there with a girl, but even then the girl seemed available, so I imagine they were sharing the profits.

A number of people I met in these clubs spoke English well enough that we could converse. And I learned a strange thing: During the German occupation every one of them had been in the Resistance, doing difficult work at extreme risk, with many companions having been captured and never seen again. These things were spoken of in low voices with an air of mystery, so it had developed into a minor art form. I remember thinking that if the Resistance workers were half so numerous as their claims implied, it was surprising that they needed help in liberating France. Of course there were genuine heroes in the Resistance, and plenty of them, but I doubt that they were telling strangers about it in Parisian night clubs. In any event, this was not my scene, as the saying would go nowadays.

I was again billeted at the Lafayette Club near the Opera House, and we were quite a distance away in Place Pigalle, where most of the Paris night clubs were located. During the evening all of my companions dropped off to stay longer at one club or another, so I was finally left alone. This had not been anticipated and posed something of a dilemma. Wartime Paris was not a safe place to be alone at night, especially since there was a blackout of all outside lighting. There was only a little light from the sky, and the streets were quite narrow. So I started walking toward my hotel in the middle of the streets, to be as far as possible from anyone in one of the dark, recessed doorways along the sides. It was about 1:00 A.M., so I didn't see any vehicles or anyone else walking in either direction; but neither were the streets exactly empty. Every now and then I was startled by the glow of a cigarette in one of the recessed doorways. Whenever this happened I watched the cigarette closely in case it started moving toward me. Those cigarettes made for an eerie experience because I was being watched most of the way, but I never saw any of the watchers. It was like running a gauntlet without knowing if I would be attacked, and if so, when or where or by whom. In any case, I felt extremely vulnerable but could only keep walking, while attempting to look much more confident than I felt.

There were only a few street signs, so navigation was also a problem, and this was no time to get lost. I don't remember how I finally found the Lafayette Club, but it was probably by walking as straight as possible in the right general direction, then picking up prominent landmarks in the vicinity of the Opera House. I remember thinking what an irony it would be to get my head bashed in under those conditions. Nothing happened, but it was a great relief to be safely back at the hotel.

The following night, Chapin and I went to the Folies Bergère, about which my next letter home enthused, "I've never seen such clever and beautiful staging. I've never seen such beautiful costumes. And I'm sure that nowhere have I ever seen such graceful dancing."

What I remember best of all about Paris, however, was the feeling of walking down the Champs Élysèes toward the Arc de Triomphe, a feeling like no other I have known. I felt exalted and uplifted, but most of all that this was the center of the world, around which everything else revolved. A palpable excitement pervaded the air and was visible in the faces around me. It was a feeling that almost anything could happen and that whatever happened would be right and good. No wonder so many fall in love in Paris. I can't explain it and would rather not try. But it was exhilarating beyond words, it was real, and I believe it was found at its best right there, and never so strongly as at that time.

Chapter 13
Crescendo to Christmas: The Battle of the Bulge

Though our October and November missions were relatively uneventful, December proved different. On the twelfth we flew my tenth mission in Ken Chapin's crew, which was the two-hundredth mission of the 391st Bomb Group. Our target was the defended German town of Harperscheid, and the attack was led by pathfinders. The first box bombed successfully that way, but we were in the second box, and our pathfinder's equipment failed. So our box bombed a nearby secondary target that proved visible through the weather. It was the center of Mayen, a communication hub through which supplies and reinforcements were being fed to Wehrmacht forces at Aachen, where our ground forces had been stalled for some time. Our strike was also successful because hits with 500-pound bombs were recorded on roads and buildings in the center of town.

After dropping our bombs we turned immediately, as we always did, to renew evasive action. As we turned, I leaned far forward to observe the bomb impacts. Then I did something I can't remember doing on any other occasion. The bombardier's seat was a kind of metal bench upon which we sat astride, and it had no backrest. So after watching the bomb impacts, I leaned far backward for a few moments of relaxation in an almost reclining position. During those few moments, a flak shell burst in front of the nose, slightly low and to the left. It was well known that if one could see the red center of a flak burst, it was within fifteen feet. This one was bright red and almost deafening. Immediately afterward, I felt prickly burning sensations on the backs of my hands, which were lying folded in my lap. I thought my hands had been sprayed with small flak fragments, but when I looked they showed no wounds of any kind.

Later I sorted out what had happened. Lodged among some equipment behind my right shoulder, I found a jagged flak fragment that I still have. It is about three-fourths of an inch long, with nasty-looking teeth, so it must have come from a threaded part of the flak shell. It had passed through the lower left of the Plexiglas nose and then through a heavy canvas bag hanging under my machine gun. This gun was normally turned aside and stored to the left, and the canvas bag was to catch empty cartridge cases as they were ejected during firing, thus preventing them from cluttering the nose space. When I examined the hole through this bag, its edges were charred, which explained what had happened to my hands. The flak fragment must have shattered the material into small burning fragments, some of which were sprayed upon the backs of my hands—and being so small, they had burned up and disappeared before I looked to see what had happened. Ken Chapin also had a close call from the same flak burst. A fragment entered his side of the cockpit, passed just under his left knee, then rattled around under him for some time before coming to rest.

The next day we went together to examine the plane in more detail. When Ken looked under his seat, there was the piece of flak, about an inch long and looking very wicked. After looking around again in the nose, I stood outside *The Ginnie Gee* and sighted through the hole in the Plexiglas to where the flak had lodged behind my right shoulder. This line of sight passed through the very center of where the bombardier would normally have been sitting. Though my body would have been protected by the flak vest, I could easily have been wounded in the arm, or even killed by a wound to the head, had I not been leaning far backward when the flak burst occurred.

It may seem surprising that our plane was not shot down by such a close burst. In practice, however, this almost always required a direct hit, and sometimes even that was insufficient. We were also fortunate that this burst was a little low. The shrapnel from a flak burst took the general form of a mushroom, the force of the explosion being expended mainly sideways and downward, with less force in the upward direction. If this burst had been a few feet higher it could easily have killed or wounded not only myself but also both Ken and Don.

Between December 12 and 23 our group flew only two missions. This was a time of exceptionally bad weather and was wisely chosen by the Germans for their buildup and counterattack in the Ardennes, which became known as The Battle of the Bulge. Our group flew missions on the thirteenth and fifteenth, and the German attack opened on the sixteenth. Their timing could not have been better because this was the first day of a period of extremely heavy fog and clouds that lasted until the twenty-third. In consequence, their attack proceeded for a full week with no opposition from bombers or fighters, which was crucial to their initial success. This was frustrating for us because it was a situation where B-26s could excel in decent weather, but we were impotent. We were even put on the defensive, because German paratroopers were being dropped behind our lines in locations as far west as Paris.

Rumors were rampant, and we had to prepare for the worst. Since no troops were available to help us, we guarded the air base ourselves. The barracks for aircrew officers of the 572d Squadron was especially vulnerable, since it was in an open field and isolated from all the rest of our bomb group. Hence a guard of our barracks was mounted on four-hour shifts. We were armed only with pistols, which seemed like a pitiful effort—but it was the best we could do. Night guard duty was the worst, and I remember peering into the fog and wondering what we could do if attacked. Raise the alarm, perhaps, but little more. One man who saw a pair of eyes staring out of the fog almost blew his cool and fired at it, but he finally realized it was only a dog. Though we were normally too far behind the lines to hear artillery, this counter-offensive reached close enough that we heard it clearly, a constant reminder of our situation. Fortunately, the rumored German paratroopers did not show up.

On the morning of December 23, the weather finally cleared enough for our group to go into action on a mission formed from squadrons other than our own. Our group's function in this battle was almost entirely the disruption of communications and supply routes to the German troops. This first mission of thirty planes was thus sent, without fighter escort, to destroy a railroad viaduct in Ahrweiler. Apparently the Germans anticipated this kind of bombing and were very concerned about its effects upon the battle. In any event, they chose this moment for the Luftwaffe's "swan song" and threw much of what they had managed to save against this one mission. About sixty German fighters attacked from the rear in a formation fifteen abreast and four deep. Sixteen of our thirty planes were shot down, twelve others were badly damaged, and many returning aircrew were wounded. Although the odds were overwhelming, our crews fought back so effectively that sixteen German fighters were destroyed, three were probably destroyed, and sixteen were damaged. In summary, it was one of the great aerial battles of the war and probably the greatest of all for B-26s.

In spite of the terrible losses, our group flew another mission that afternoon. The target was Neuerburg, a defended village and communication center important to the Ardennes offensive. It was likewise bombed effectively and the Luftwaffe did not appear, nor did it ever again show up in force.

As my name was not on the ready list for either mission that day, I could only wander around the air base looking at the damaged planes and learning what had happened. Although no one in our squadron had been involved, and no one that I knew was killed or wounded, it seemed very personal. The extent of the destruction was hard to believe, and it could have happened just as easily to our squadron.

The next day, December 24, I was on a mission to Konz-Karthaus, a center for supply lines to the attacking German forces. There we successfully bombed railroad lines and a railway bridge without losses or casualties. That evening, Christmas Eve, I think we all felt very lonely and far from home, especially after our group's heavy losses the day before. Though our squadron was on call for two missions the next day, we had been assured the weather would not permit any flying. So many of us decided this was an ideal time to break out supplies from the seven-bottle deal and do some serious drinking. Once begun, it continued far into the night, and I became drunk for the first time. The second time was after my own worst mission, and only one other occurred during all the years of my later life.

Contrary to prediction, and to the dismay of almost everyone on the morning mission, Christmas Day dawned clear and cold. I thanked my lucky stars not to be on that mission, being too sick and tired to function well. In spite of many aircrew on that mission being in similar condition, Bitburg was bombed with outstanding success. This was another German communications center and supply route to the Ardennes. There were no losses or casualties, but thirteen planes were damaged by flak. The success of that morning mission was surely a tribute to the resilience of youth. I marveled at it myself but was fully recovered for the afternoon mission. We attacked a rail bridge at Taben—with results rated excellent—and returned without losses, damage, or casualties. What a way to spend Christmas!

The next day I was on our final mission that was part of the Ardennes counteroffensive. Forty-seven planes were sent to bomb a rail bridge in Bad Münster, likewise with excellent results, several additional bridges and other targets also being destroyed. Two planes were damaged by flak, and one had to crash land at our base when its nose wheel failed to lower.

In summary, I participated in three of the six missions flown by our group during the Battle of the Bulge, and our operations were judged highly effective in defeating that counteroffensive. In official recognition of this fact, the 391st Bombardment Group was awarded what is often called a Presidential Unit Citation, more formally described as a Distinguished Unit Citation by the War Department for "...outstanding performance of duty in action against the enemy from 23 to 26 December 1944."

As 1944 came to a close, I thought of what a full and exciting year it had been. I had become a bombardier-navigator and then trained with a B-26 crew, with which I had flown the northern route to the ETO, joined the 391st Bomb Group, and experienced my first few months of combat. During my early missions I hadn't felt that my contributions were very significant. But after the Battle of the Bulge, I had at least become part of an effort that contributed significantly to Allied success in one of the crucial battles of World War II. So I gave thanks for the blessings of 1944, both to myself and to the Allied cause, upon which the future of our world so strongly depended.

Chapter 14

The New Year

January 1945 proved a downslide from the crescendo of action that peaked at Christmas. Winter weather set in with a vengeance, including much snow and ice, which kept the ground crews shoveling snow from around the planes, in addition to extra maintenance of the engines. Our ground personnel were so efficient that operations were limited little, if at all, by problems with the aircraft or airfield. It was mainly the poor flying weather that kept us on the ground. As a result, the entire group flew only seven missions in January, of which I was on two.

At that time our ground forces were approaching the Rhine River, and we began bombing bridges over the Rhine to aid them. Cutting these bridges interrupted the main enemy supply lines and also interfered with the German retreat. These bridges were not anticipated to aid Allied troops upon reaching the Rhine, because they were expected to be blown anyway by the retreating enemy forces.

As part of this major effort, we were sent on January 16 to bomb the famous three-span Hermann Göring highway bridge, which crossed the Rhine at Neuwied. We had five flights of planes, and because of the small target we bombed visually by flights. From the nose of our plane, my views were always outstanding in every direction except to the rear, providing the weather was clear. On this mission it was indeed clear, exceptionally so for that time, and a great relief after struggling with so much cloudy weather. It was always exciting to watch the land as it unfolded beneath us, especially while over Germany, where gunfire from flak batteries might erupt at any moment. But the day was so bright and beautiful that I felt optimistic and unburdened by grim thoughts. As we approached Neuwied, we were too high for a good view of the bridge. I learned later that it was exceptionally beautiful, but thankfully I wasn't aware of that at the time.

Although considerable flak was encountered at the target, it didn't interfere with our flight's bomb run. After releasing our 2,000-pound bombs, I watched carefully as they made several direct hits on the bridge. This was something I hadn't seen before with such a crucial target, and the resulting exultation was so strong it is hard to describe. My emotion must have resulted partly from the visible culmination, in one brief moment, of all the months of training and waiting for such a success as this. But I also knew the importance to our ground forces of bringing down that bridge. In any event, I have never felt anything else quite like that critical moment.

Our flight and one other were officially credited with direct hits. Later reconnaissance photos showed that both the eastern and the western spans were dropped into the Rhine, and a high overpass was also taken out on the eastern side. Four of our planes were damaged by flak, and when one of these crashed, two crewmen were killed and four injured.

Seven years after the war, Ginnie and I toured Europe together. Most of the minor damage had been repaired by that time, but much of the major destruction was still evident. When we took a steamer down the Rhine, passing Neuwied was an emotional experience for me because the bridge was still in the river. Though I had exulted in destroying it, thus completing our assigned task, that seemed a hollow victory in 1952 as the bridge still lay in ugly rubble, so I deeply regretted the necessities that had brought it down. Such are the ironies and mixed emotions made inevitable by war.

By early 1945 I was convinced that the B-26, contrary to its early reputation, was one of the safest planes in which to serve, owing mainly to the ruggedness of its construction and the excellence of its pilots. For myself, this had been illustrated best by an extraordinary incident on December 2, 1944, to which I may have been the only nearby eyewitness on the ground.

After lunch that day I was alone and walking parallel with the runway on the road back to our barracks from the mess hall. There was a typical low overcast hanging only about a hundred feet above the ground. A morning mission had been flown by other squadrons, and I thought all the planes had returned. But I began hearing a plane, which soon appeared just under the overcast, dead on course for the runway. None of the wheels was down, so I watched closely, and as it came abreast I had a strong impression of looking *through* the plane. Its belly landing was perfect, with the forward section making contact first, thus lifting the tail safely away from the runway.

This plane proved to be from the 573rd squadron, so I didn't know any of the crew, and during the war I only learned details through the stories that circulated in our barracks. However, early printings of this book evoked contacts from both the pilot, Edmund B. Dunn, and the copilot, Edwin H. Armstrong, who provided written accounts and lengthy telephone interviews, upon which the following details are based.

The mission's target was an oil depot at Saarlautern, Germany, for which each plane carried sixteen 250-pound fragmentation bombs, and Dunn's crew was flying the No. 4(slot) position in one of the three flights. As the target was approached, the clouds below parted briefly, exposing the formation of 18 planes to intense flak. During this barrage an 88mm flak shell entered Dunn's rear bomb bay just below the top turret, blowing the plane almost in half. It blew away the top turret and at least six feet of the catwalk, which was an I-beam providing the only strong structural connection to the tail. This left the tail attached only by the plane's remaining aluminum "skin," namely, that near the top turret plus some on the left side. Of course this material was quite thin, intended as an outer covering with little or no planned role in connecting the tail.

Only a few moments after the direct hit, another flak shell burst slightly below and to the left of the pilot's compartment. Numerous fragments from this burst sprayed upward into the cockpit, badly wounding Dunn in both the right ankle and right elbow. This second burst must have been close indeed because Dunn says it felt as if his body was struck by a sledge hammer, and he was briefly knocked unconscious, undoubtedly direct effects of the concussion. This burst also shattered or rendered inoperative many of the instruments, leaving only the needle-ball, magnetic compass, airspeed indicator and altimeter. Both Armstrong and Hartwell, who was in the nose, were unscathed. Hartwell was a sergeant trained as a toggleier for duty in non-lead crews, and this was his first and only mission with Dunn's crew.

Shortly after the flak bursts, Armstrong recalls "...pushing the nose of the plane down to maintain air speed, and with throttles and ailerons [turning] out of formation and back toward our lines." When Dunn recovered consciousness, he says that both of them working together could not move the rudder. So all rudder control was lost, and they could steer only by using the throttles to play the engines against each other. Elevator control was also much impaired, since only one of the four control cables to the elevators had survived the direct hit. Fortunately, however, the aileron controls were intact. Though blood was flowing from his right boot and jacket sleeve, Dunn took over the controls. Soon thereafter, Armstrong says he called Hartwell "...out of the nose to take care of Ed's wounds and to give him a shot of morphine because I didn't want Ed to go into shock." Of course this could not have been done without Dunn flying the plane, because the bombardier could not exit from the nose unless the copilot left his seat or moved it as far back as possible, well away from the controls. Indeed, the entire flight home proved an outstanding example of what could be attained by two pilots who had learned to trust each other and to work together in close coordination.

Since the intercom was out, Armstrong went back to inspect conditions in the tail. Upon entering the bomb bay, he first noted that the entire tail was swaying from side to side with an excursion of at least a foot in each direction. He also noted that the bombs, which had been armed for the bomb run by having their pins removed, were all blown askew in their racks. So the bombs were in a very hazardous condition. But they could not be salvoed for several reasons, most notably because the hydraulically operated bomb bay doors could not be opened.

The top turret with its gunner, Ellerbe, was almost entirely blown away. This was especially tragic because Ellerbe was also not part of Dunn's regular crew, having joined them only for this mission, his 65th, to complete his tour of duty. The waist gunner, James B. Sims, was riddled with fragments, one of which had severed his spinal cord, so he was helpless and in critical condition. It was discovered later that some of his wounds were caused by flak fragments, and others resulted from pieces of the plane blasted into him. The tail gunner, John J. Wagner, was also wounded but much less severely. In spite of his own wounds, he had thoughtfully attached a line to Sims's ripcord. If bailout had been ordered, he planned to push Sims out first and pull the ripcord for him, since Sims could not have done it himself.

When Armstrong returned to the cockpit, the pilots rejected the usual solution under such circumstances, namely, bailout as soon as they were over friendly territory. Instead, since it was the only possibility of saving Sims, they decided to attempt flying the plane all the way back to Roye/Ami. In the tail, Wagner could have considered Sims a lost cause and bailed out on his own, but he didn't. Thus their only chance of survival was a successful belly landing with the nose section making contact first. If the tail touched first, as could easily happen with such badly damaged flight controls, the tail section would break off and they would both be killed in a high speed tumble down the runway. Sims may not have thought about this, but Wagner almost certainly did, so his trip home must have been "a real sweat job," an apt phrase that was used by our aircrews to describe such highly stressful situations.

Having decided to fly home, Dunn and Armstrong had a serious problem with navigation. Their entire electrical system was out, including the radio, so they could not communicate with other planes or with ground bases. Also Hartwell, their toggleier, had no training in navigation, and the ground was obscured by solid clouds below their altitude of about 7000 ft. So they could only take an approximate compass heading back to Roye/Ami and let down through the clouds, hoping to navigate the remaining distance by pilotage.

Their letdown took over an hour because it had to be done very slowly to avoid hitting the ground before they saw it. When the altimeter registered zero, the ground had still not appeared, so they had to let down even more carefully. Finally they saw the ground dimly through the clouds and rain, when their true altitude was only about 100 feet. The terrain was strange to both of them, but they were flying in a valley through which a canal was flowing. Armstrong studied the map and decided they were over the Oise Canal, so he gave Dunn a heading to the northwest where Roye/Ami should be, at a distance of about 100 miles. Since hills were expected along this course, Dunn went back up to 1000 ft, having reset the altimeter from ground level. After half an hour, they let down again and broke out in misty rain with an airstrip not far ahead. But the runway proved to be full of huge bomb craters. However, Armstrong spotted two railroad tracks, one of which he thought would lead them to Roye/Ami, and indeed it did. They first knew they were in the right area when they spotted a familiar chapel, from which the airfield was only a bit southeast. One can only imagine their emotions upon seeing that chapel and realizing they had a chance to survive. The flight home had taken over two hours, but a demanding and critical task was still ahead. Since some of their hydraulic lines were severed, the flaps could not be lowered, forcing the landing speed to be even greater than normal. And the wheels could not be let down, so it had to be a belly landing. Dunn says they touched down at about 160 mph and then slid about 4,000 ft.

Miraculously, they had avoided all of the disasters which could have occurred beyond their control. The tail had not fallen off from turbulence during the long flight home, and it even held during the unavoidable stress of their belly landing. Also, although the 16 armed bombs were very dangerous, especially during the landing, not one of them exploded; nor did the plane catch fire. And when the whirling propeller blades hit the runway, they only bent harmlessly backward, instead of breaking off and slicing into the cockpit—always a hazard to pilots during a belly landing.

Sims was taken immediately to the base infirmary, after which he was hospitalized. He was incurably paralyzed and suffered terribly from his wounds. Even so, months later he asked his family to write to Dunn for him, expressing heartfelt thanks for his life having been saved. And two years after his fateful mission, this indomitable man finally succumbed to his wounds.

In recognition of their extraordinary feat, Dunn received the Distinguished Service Cross, our nation's second highest military award, and Armstrong received the Distinguished Flying Cross. What those wartime B-26 pilots could do has never ceased to astonish me; no wonder that after the war, airlines snapped them up like hotcakes. This is also the best example from my experience of the extreme damage a B-26 could sustain and still bring us back. In his history of the 391st Bombardment Group, Hugh Walker says this plane was "....beyond a doubt the most battle damaged B-26 airplane to fly home."

Soon after the mission to Neuwied, my personal life was boosted by a change of quarters. The eight-man room had become wearing on my nerves, mainly because the garrulous, unpleasant fellow was in the top bunk right above mine. I had longed to move into a smaller four-man room, and the chance finally came when a veteran crew finished its tour of missions. This permitted Ken Chapin, Don Fry, and me to move in with Bill Netherton, a lead navigator who was nearing his sixty-fifth mission. This made a congenial group, so my life in the barracks became much more pleasant.

This pleasure was soon overshadowed, however, by a "Dear John" letter, the classic news so dreaded by servicemen. At Miami University in Oxford, Ohio, about nine months before entering the service, I had met the only girl I had been serious about until that time. Our relationship had seemed almost ideal, and it had been furthered since by correspondence. Thus the one thing that had most sustained my spirits had been looking forward to life with her after the war. But she had suddenly married an old friend, a Marine captain who was home on leave after going through the entire campaign on Guadalcanal. The pressures of combat made me especially vulnerable to this kind of hurt, so it was a bad time. However, I finally realized that if this could occur, we never should have married. Indeed, I even came to think of it as a blessing in disguise.

---

*Amazingly, among the eleven pilots with whom I flew in combat, two became chief pilots of major airlines after the war. Preben Bonde became known as "P.K." at United Airlines, in which he became Vice-President of Flight Operations, in addition to Chief Pilot of the Western Division. And Dana Wetherbee became a Chief Pilot with American Airlines.

Chapter 15

How I Became a Lead Navigator—by Mistake

At the end of January I had flown sixteen missions, in all of which I had functioned as the bombardier-navigator in non-lead planes. This meant I had no role in bomb aiming, only releasing bombs with a toggle switch when bombs fell from the lead plane of our flight. This was often referred to as being a "toggleier," and it carried little responsibility for the success or failure of a mission, hence little satisfaction. Similarly, my work as navigator was almost entirely as backup to the lead navigator of our flight, in case our plane should become separated from the flight. That happened only once, the time we had to return on a single engine—but the pilots probably could have found our airfield on their own. So I was risking my life to little purpose and often felt I was just along for the ride.

My role changed dramatically, however, when I was tapped to become a lead navigator in early February 1945. By that time I realized that becoming a top-notch lead bombardier required an especially rare type of personality that I didn't have. From the beginning, however, I had been keen on navigation and had become proficient in it. Apparently my abilities were correctly assessed by Major Joe Earll, our squadron operations officer, who chose all of the lead pilots, bombardiers, and navigators. This new assignment was much appreciated, and it was the ironic culmination of a long story.

Back in the classification center at Nashville, I had requested navigation as my specialty. However, at that time no one was sent to navigation school unless a minor physical defect prevented him from becoming a bombardier or pilot. One could become a bombardier by choice, as I did, but the powers-that-be made it clear that they preferred I become a pilot. Thus, the functions of the classification center were rendered largely irrelevant by an overriding policy of training huge numbers of pilots, only a few bombardiers, and almost no navigators. I wondered from the beginning what could be the reason for this decision, since bombing was expected to play a major role in World War II. So I watched as the adverse results of this policy unfolded in several stages and became a serious limitation to efficient uses of manpower during latter stages of the air war. Although some pieces of this story have already been mentioned, it seems worthwhile to put them together here in the sequence in which they occurred.

By the time I completed bombardier school, bombardiers were in such short supply that some of us were graduated early on a crash basis, for some purpose we never knew because the plan was either altered or dropped. Next, upon starting operational training in B-26s, the crew I joined had been waiting around doing nothing for several weeks because of not being able to proceed without a bombardier-navigator. This was at Barksdale Field, which also served as a "replacement depot" where pilots awaited assignments for operational training in specific types of planes. With pilots being turned out in such large numbers, Barksdale was flooded with them because of insufficient facilities for their further training. Hence there were rows and rows of barracks, all occupied by pilots with nothing to do. Later, when I joined the 391st Bomb Group, all of the lead navigators had gone through navigation school and become fully rated navigators. While at Roye/Ami, many of them were completing their tours of missions and going home, and they couldn't be replaced with rated navigators because none was available. So I was made a lead navigator. This wouldn't have been possible if celestial navigation had been required in our operations. However, we used only pilotage and dead reckoning, plus GEE, in which bombardier-navigators had as much training as fully rated navigators. Thus, I became a lead navigator by the mistake of a policy that led to insufficient rated navigators.

There is a sequel to this story. After the war I obtained a Ph.D. in physiological psychology, then began four years as a research psychologist in the Aeromedical Laboratory at Wright-Patterson Air Force Base near Dayton, Ohio. The head of the psychology section of that laboratory, who hired me and became my superior, was Walter Grether. Soon after Ginnie and I arrived, he invited us home for dinner, after which we reminisced about experiences in the service. Thinking to amuse him, I related my ironic story about becoming a lead navigator. Instead he looked grave and finally said, "You know, I was the one who designed that classification program." I feel sure he designed it only from a technical standpoint and had nothing to do with overriding military policy. But of course I couldn't say that.

The new assignment at Roye/Ami changed my situation greatly. For example, instead of the great visibility from the plane's nose, I now had only limited visibility through a small window on the right side of the navigator's compartment. However, I had much more time to think and plan. So I saw less but thought more, and the additional responsibility was very satisfying.

Equally or more important were dramatic changes in my relations with other members of our aircrews. A newly assigned lead pilot went into that position with his own copilot, enlisted crewmen, and sometimes his original bombardier. But some lead bombardiers and all lead navigators were more like free agents, being assigned where they were needed in the lead crews of each mission.

Chapin became a lead pilot, and shortly thereafter I served as his navigator on two missions. In both cases, we led the element of planes carrying window. But these were my last missions with Chapin's crew. We had become like a family, and I missed them. However, every lead crew was a core family, with only the navigator and sometimes the bombardier as visitors. And all members of lead crews, including the visitors, were sufficiently experienced and confident that we trusted each other, so I found it easy and natural to move from one lead crew to another. All told, I flew with ten different lead crews, and we always worked well together. This may seem unlikely, because a comparable situation might be difficult to find in peacetime civilian life. However, during World War II the entire country, military and civilian alike, was pulling together toward a common goal in a way rarely, if ever, seen before or since.

My new assignment also led to new associations, some of which became quite strong. Ed Wegenek had joined our squadron rather recently, and he became a lead bombardier almost immediately. His origins were Polish and he was short and stocky, thus a perfect fit for the nose of a B-26, and his background for lead bombardier was exceptional. Unlike all of our other bombardiers, he was a career army officer instead of a reservist, and after bombardier training he had spent a year as an instructor. He was also older than most of us and already a first lieutenant when he arrived. After a few early misses, while getting used to combat, he quickly became recognized as a very talented bombardier. Soon after I became a lead navigator, we flew together on several missions, and the combination seemed to click. Apparently this was recognized because thereafter we were usually assigned together to whatever lead crew needed us. We not only worked well together but became good friends, often going together when we had free time away from the air bases we used after leaving Roye/Ami.

Soon after Wegenek and I became a team, we started flying with Preben Bonde, a pilot then known as just "Bonde." Born in Denmark, he had been raised from age four on a farm in Colorado, to which his family had migrated. Reflecting his Danish ancestry, he was tall, blond, and handsome, like a latter-day Viking or a Hollywood version of what a pilot should look like. But that was only the surface. Underneath he was all business—competent, trustworthy, and calm under stress. During advanced twin-engine training, he had requested assignment to the P-38 Lightning, the most advanced fighter plane of that time. Instead, he was sent for transition training in the B-25 Mitchell. Like Wegenek, after completing his own training he stayed on as an instructor, training replacement pilots for B-25s in the Pacific Theater. This type of duty soon became routine for him, so when volunteers were solicited for the A-26 Invader in Europe, he jumped at the chance. However, upon arriving in the 391st Bomb Group on the day Myers was killed, he learned that A-26s were not available and he would be a replacement pilot in B-26s—a plane he had never even seen before. He was quickly checked out with a few takeoffs and landings, taken on two missions as Brockway's copilot, then sent into combat as pilot and commander of a plane and crew. When we first flew together about five months later, he had already become highly respected. Thereafter, I flew with him on nine missions, many more than with any other pilot during my twenty-seven missions as a lead navigator. More important, he was the pilot on all three of my most noteworthy missions in that capacity. So Bonde, Wegenek, and I went through a great deal together.

Chapter 16

Operation CLARION

Typical of things to come, my first mission with Bonde was unusual, so much so that it had a special name, Operation CLARION. We had been briefed for this operation about a month earlier by a general from the 9th Bombardment Division. Apparently he briefed each squadron separately, because I still remember him briefing aircrew officers of the 572d Squadron in our barracks one evening, while sitting on a table with one foot on the floor and the other leg swinging casually back and forth.

He said Operation CLARION was going to be a combined operation of all Allied aircraft in the ETO. On every mission we would be expected to bomb and then go down to strafe, something we had never even been allowed to do before. Most impressive of all, he said we would be flying two missions a day, and that we would continue to do this *"until all the planes and men are used up."* Perhaps he was being overly dramatic to impress us. If so, he certainly succeeded. He said the purpose of this operation was an all-out aerial offensive to speed the end of the war, especially by convincing the Germans, military and civilian alike, that further resistance was useless.

After this briefing everyone was very sober because it sounded like an operation few of us would survive. While using up the Germans, we were also being told we would use up ourselves. Many letters were written home that night, some including last wishes or wills, in case these were the last letters we would write. Although we hadn't been given the operation's timing, we were told to expect it soon.

Then, as so often occurs in military service, nothing happened. When this had gone on for several weeks, we thought Operation CLARION had been scrubbed. Finally, in the early morning darkness of February 22, those of us on flying alert were awakened to be taken for briefing, and we were told that even if there were long delays after briefing, we would not be allowed to return to the barracks. Since that instruction was unprecedented, we felt sure this mission would be the beginning of Operation CLARION.

When we reached the operations building the sky had become reasonably light, and believe it or not, a workman was already up on a ladder painting the building. Furthermore, his ladder stood in front of the door in such a manner that it was easy enough to enter by walking under the ladder, but otherwise it was difficult. Out of curiosity, I stopped awhile to see what would happen. Though I doubt if any of us would have admitted to being superstitious, during the considerable period I watched *not one man* walked under the ladder.

If challenged to explain this, I imagine the reasoning would run somewhat as follows. I once heard a story (probably apocryphal) of a visitor to a scientist's office who noticed a rabbit's foot on the desk. Unable to control his curiosity, the visitor asked whether the scientist really believed in that kind of thing. The indignant reply was, "Of course not, but I understand it works whether one believes in it or not." So how did I enter the building? Like everyone else, of course. With Operation CLARION only a few hours away, this was no time to take chances. After all, the workman might have dropped his bucket of paint on me.

The tactical objective of B-26s in Operation CLARION was maximum disruption of the railway system. Thus, we were sent in three complete boxes to bomb railroad bridges in three small towns, plus a railroad platform and roundhouse in Marburg. Bombing by flights, we had two flights for each railroad bridge and three for Marburg. Each flight was given the option to strafe targets of opportunity after bombing, which all flights did, breaking up to allow every plane to strafe separately. Although this was the only time our bomb group ever strafed, it was something for which B-26s were well qualified, having the speed of a fighter plane but much more firepower, including four fixed forward-firing guns, three gunners with two machine guns each, and the bombardier's flexible nose gun.

The target of our flight was a railroad bridge at Altenhunden. Following our bomb run and observing the results, we went into a steep dive, during which our airspeed climbed to about 350 miles per hour. This was an astonishing speed for a bomber in those days, and this speed was maintained through the strafing run, during which all the other crew members fired at anything that looked useful to the Germans, especially communications or transport. As the only crew member without a machine gun, I could only watch, but as we flew through Altenhunden we were so low and so fast that everything went by in a blur. Though one might think that the forward firing of so many guns would have noticeably slowed the plane, apparently this was prevented by the weight and speed of the plane. But the noise from the firing was horrific. After strafing, we climbed back to altitude as rapidly as possible, being vulnerable to many kinds of enemy fire at low altitudes, and our flight re-formed for the return home.

Among the nine flights on this mission, bombing results were rated excellent for two and superior for the other seven, which included our own. This resulted in the following commendation from General Anderson to the 391st Bomb Group: "Your results on Operation CLARION were grand. I congratulate and commend you most highly and wish you continued success.... You surpassed your reputation for outstanding aggressiveness, initiative, and accuracy." In spite of results like these, or perhaps because of them, the participation of B-26s in Operation CLARION thankfully terminated after this one mission. However, the operation continued one more day, February 23, with massive attacks by heavy bombers and fighters of the Eighth Air Force.

Chapter 17

The Ordeal by Flak of Flight 4

During the afternoon of February 24, only two days after Operation CLARION, Bonde, Wegenek, and I led a flight of planes that went through an incredible experience.

It began routinely enough, as a mission of twenty-seven planes to bomb a railroad bridge at Irlich, Germany—considerably farther beyond the bomb line than most of our targets. Our formation was a single box of four flights, of which we were the fourth. Our trip to Irlich was uneventful, but the target area was defended by heavy and accurate flak, and matters were made much worse by a line of low clouds running north to south near the bridge. As we began our bomb run on an easterly course, as planned, we had enough visual references to get lined up. However, we couldn't tell whether, after passing over the clouds, we would see the target soon enough to bomb it. This could be determined only by risking the flak and making the bomb run on speculation. That is what we did, but it proved a losing gamble.

In Flight 1, Clarence Martin was flying the slot position directly behind his flight leader, who was also leading the entire mission. They were on the bomb run with heavy flak bursting all around when Martin saw the lead plane suddenly explode into a fireball near the root of the right wing. Although still in one piece at that point, the lead B-26 was burning fiercely and immediately started down. It must have taken a direct hit that exploded the right wing tank, which was located where Martin saw the flames. This plane was piloted by Captain Burton Hanisch, one of the handful of West Point graduates in our bomb group. I never met him because he was in a different squadron, but he must have been highly respected to be designated the mission leader. There were eyewitness reports of a plane going down with its right wing shot off. That plane was probably Hanisch's, because his right wing likely burned off or broke off soon after the plane began its vertical descent.

Martin's copilot, Arlo Sienknecht, also saw the brilliant flash and instantly felt a wave of intense heat sweep over his plane. In fact, it was so intense they later learned it had burned all the fabric from their control surfaces on the right side. This included not only the right aileron and elevator but also the centrally located rudder. Though an aluminum "skin" covered the rigid parts of a B-26, the control surfaces were covered by heavily doped fabric, which burned much more readily. Debris from the exploding gas tank must have been minimal because neither pilot heard any clattering against their plane, nor did they find any debris damage later. In any event, their plane went out of control and into a spin, from which Martin somehow recovered. He then jettisoned the bombs and ordered bailout, but no one left the plane, electing instead to ride it down. This was regarded as a personal choice and was not uncommon. They headed west toward home, with their progress slowed by the bomb bay doors being stuck open. The plane again went out of control, and again they recovered. By then it was getting dark and fog was rolling in, so Martin made a belly landing in the French countryside. The bombardier had been wounded in the leg by flak, but no one was hurt in the crash landing, and within a few days they were all back at work at our air base.

Orville (Ike) Cambier was piloting plane number 6 at the left rear corner of this lead flight. He reports that when the lead plane was hit, there was such a "terrific explosion" that he instinctively made an immediate left turn out of formation. Without a flight leader, and having no bombsight of his own, he was unable to bomb effectively, and he couldn't find the remnants of his flight. So he returned to base alone. Ike also reports a wave of extreme heat when Hanisch was hit, but no clattering of debris, and he learned later that the heat had burned off much of his plane's paint.

Another flight (either the second or third) was even harder hit. Paul Young was flying on the left wing of his flight leader (the number 3 position), with Stuart Main (Stu) directly behind him in the left rear corner of the flight (number 6). This gave Stu an excellent view of what happened, which he recorded in his diary a few days later. Just after the IP his bombardier, Ed Clark, suffered a compound skull fracture from a chunk of flak. This same burst, or another at about the same time, damaged his left engine. Soon thereafter he saw Paul Young's plane take a direct hit in the nose and drop out of the formation. About a minute later, the plane on the flight leader's right (number 2), flown by Captain G. T. McPherson, also took a direct hit; most of the left wing was blown off, and the plane spun in. Before Paul's plane was hit, his tail gunner had been watching as the plane on Stu's right (number 5) was likewise hit; it exploded on the way down, and there was no sign of survivors. This was the only plane shot down during this mission whose pilot I have been unable to identify from eyewitness reports. However, it must have been Lieutenant W. M. Huskey, whose plane also failed to return from this mission.

With his damaged left engine, Stu was soon forced to leave the formation and head home. About halfway back, the engine caught fire and he had to feather it. Though their bombs had been salvoed over enemy territory, his plane steadily lost altitude on the single engine. So he ordered his crew to throw out everything heavy that they could, and he then managed to fly back to Roye/Ami, which may have saved the bombardier's life by getting medical attention as soon as possible. Stu was awarded the DFC.

Meanwhile, when Paul Young's plane was hit, the explosion blew off the nose containing the bombardier and killed the copilot with severe head wounds. It also blew off the entire top of the cockpit and destroyed the windshield and most of the instrument panel, leaving only the altimeter, airspeed indicator, and needle-ball. The blast even stripped off Paul's helmet, sunglasses, and intercom, and his head was driven so hard against the left side of the cockpit that he was knocked out. All three gunners bailed out as soon as possible, acting upon a pact to do so after a direct hit. They all survived; two evaded successfully and got back to the American lines, but the third was taken prisoner.

When Paul came to, his plane was in a spin, and both engines were on fire. He brought the plane under control by going into a dive, during which the airspeed went up to about 300 miles per hour. The airstream put out the fires, and Paul then leveled off. During the dive he must have kept his head well down in the cockpit to avoid the airstream in his face. After leveling off, he needed to see ahead, so he looked just over the remaining lower frame of the windshield, which deflected much of the airstream up and over him. However, his visibility was also hindered by glass splinters from his shattered sunglasses that had lodged in his eyes and face. It was late in the day, so he flew west by heading toward the sun. His bombs had been armed for the bomb run, and he didn't try to salvo them because they could not be disarmed. Owing to the damaged engines and full bomb load, he could not fly higher than about twenty-five hundred feet and was drawing 20mm light flak, from which he took several hits. When the light flak finally stopped for a few minutes, it seemed likely he was over the bomb line, so when he saw a promising wheat field, he circled it several times and then bellied in. His back was later found to have seven broken or crushed vertebrae. Since he couldn't walk, he avoided the danger of fire by crawling out of the plane and a few hundred yards away, where he was picked up by an American antiaircraft crew and taken to an aid station. There, a doctor spent four hours picking the glass fragments from his face and eyes.

Only two weeks before, Paul had earned a DFC for making a successful crash landing in rough country with both engines dead. Often referred to as a "deadstick" crash landing, a successful one with a B-26 was almost unheard of in rough country. For his heroic flying and outstanding valor on this latest mission, he was awarded the Silver Star.

Ken Chapin and Don Fry were flying the slot position in this flight before it was so badly shot up. Young's plane was slightly ahead and to the left, and Ken saw a great shower of debris when it was hit. In the few moments before Young spun down out of sight, Ken found himself looking directly into the cockpit, which had been blasted open. McPherson's plane was a bit ahead and to the right, and Ken was looking toward it when a direct hit, just outboard from the left engine, blew off most of the left wing. With lift from the right wing still normal and most support on the left suddenly removed, McPherson's plane went into a snap roll, a counterclockwise rotation around the axis of its fuselage. Ken says this happened so fast the plane was already upside down, with the tail pointed toward the earth, when it passed out of sight. Needless to say, Ken remembers this mission vividly, and it must have been a terrible experience for him and his crew. The planes on both sides had been stripped away by flak, leaving only himself and the flight leader. He recalls reporting to his flight leader that all the other planes were gone and he was moving to his leader's right wing. The remaining two planes thus returned to Roye/Ami, and one can only imagine the long thoughts of loss and deliverance that must have crowded the minds of their crews during that flight.

I had watched from my navigator's window as a plane with one wing shot off was going down almost vertically in a tight spin. I remember yelling silently, inside my head, "Get out, get out!" Finally, a single chute appeared—but no more. The plane was spinning so fast the centrifugal force alone must have made it almost impossible to get to an exit. And there was so little time!

The plane I watched go down must have been Hanisch's because I learned much later that his tail gunner, Valentino Rivoli, somehow managed to bail out and spent the remainder of the war in a German prison camp. I didn't learn this until July of 2003, when I no longer had any hope of identifying the parachutist I saw over Irlich. The information finally came in two letters, which arrived only 10 days apart.

As lead navigator it was my duty to choose a secondary target if the primary could not be bombed. Before the mission I had chosen a road bridge; it was some distance south, and our group had failed to destroy it on two prior missions, probably because of bad weather. After attempting to bomb the primary target, we thus turned south and were joined by a straggler, almost certainly from the leaderless first flight. Little could he know what he was getting into by joining us.

Although flak had been heavy at the target, it proved only a prelude to the ordeal that began just after we turned south. It was all tracking flak, heavy and accurate, and all aimed at us because there were no other planes nearby. We began evasive action immediately, making a turn about every fifteen seconds, but so many guns were shooting at us that the flak stayed very close, no matter what we did. After any given segment of straight flight, some gunners must have assumed we would turn left, while others assumed we would turn right. At least all the guns couldn't assume we would fly straight ahead; their flak shells had to be divided among three options, so our evasive action must have been effective in that way. However, we couldn't notice it.

Since the flak guns covered a very large area, where we had not encountered them on any other mission, I assumed until recently that they were 88mm guns mounted on German heavy tanks. But I have now learned that the tank guns could not be elevated sufficiently for use against aircraft. Instead, we must have encountered mobile guns, either towed or self-propelled, which could be fully elevated. A German armored division usually had tanks and mobile 88s in about equal numbers, the former being heavily armored and used largely for attacking fortifications, while the latter were more versatile. With greater mobility and carrying larger stocks of ammunition, those mobile 88s were very bad news for us.

After directing evasive action for a while, I turned it over to Wegenek, and we took turns until we were finally back over the bomb line. This gave me time for navigation, but the evasive action made accurate navigation impossible. During Wegenek's turns, he initially did evasive maneuvers the usual way, by timing, but he soon improvised another method for these circumstances. Since the guns were pointed at us, he could see the gun flashes clearly, and they were so frequent he began making a turn *only when there were more gun flashes than usual*. Perhaps this conveys, better than anything else, the intensity of the flak being fired at us. Wegenek's method might seem risky, and indeed it was, because many flak shells must have reached us without our having made any turn to evade them. However, everything was very risky under those conditions, and Wegenek's method seemed to work as well as the usual one.

With both methods, however, near misses were frequent. In some cases we would know a near miss by seeing the red flash in the center of a burst, which meant it was no farther away than about fifteen feet. In other cases we would feel the plane shudder or buck from a concussion we couldn't see. And all near misses, of course, were very loud. For myself, the bursts directly under us had the greatest emotional impact. Each one evoked a hollow and vaguely sick feeling in my belly. And there was something especially ominous about an explosion just underneath that seemed to say "I almost reached you this time, and the next one will be right there."

Our flight from the primary to the secondary target must have taken much longer than normal because of the constant evasive action. What with that and the flak, it seemed like an eternity before Wegenek spotted a bridge that looked like the one I had chosen. He couldn't tell whether it was actually the one chosen, or only a look-alike, but at that point we couldn't be choosy. Our southerly course was directly over the road to the bridge, and we immediately went into our bomb run.

During a bomb run there was normally nothing for the navigator to do, so I looked over Bonde's shoulder to watch the PDI. After the needle swung one direction, and Bonde made a course change, the needle almost immediately swung the other way. When this happened a couple of times, I realized Bonde was overcorrecting. Indeed, how could he not be? With all that flak and in the extreme danger of the bomb run, our brains must have been flooded with adrenaline, and the tension made delicately coordinated actions especially difficult. There was an unwritten rule that during a bomb run the intercom was left open for only the bombardier and pilot. However, I knew Wegenek was very busy, and something had to be done quickly, without undue concern for rules. So I got on the intercom and tried to help, deliberately speaking as calmly as possible while saying things such as "Okay, Bonde, let's just take it slow and easy and we'll get this right." Great pilot that he was, it seemed to be all he needed. The needle of the PDI soon settled down in dead center, indicating a perfect response to Wegenek's requested course corrections.

The story of the rest of the bomb run came from Wegenek after the mission. He said he had the crosshairs riding steadily on his aiming point at the near end of the bridge. Then, with only a few seconds to bomb release, he saw four gun flashes through the bombsight. Noting that two of these were on each side of the road, just on the other side of the bridge, he moved his crosshairs forward to the gun flashes. When the bombs released, we immediately turned west, toward home, and Wegenek watched as our pattern of twelve 2,000-pound bridge bombs, the heaviest we ever carried, completely blanketed the area of the four gun flashes. Our bombs were much more powerful than required for mobile 88s, so all four of the guns and their crews must have been destroyed. And our turn toward home took us away from their salvo of flak shells, which exploded harmlessly behind us. In the circumstances of that time, we couldn't possibly have destroyed a more satisfying target. The bomb pattern was so close to the bridge that we may have destroyed it as well, but we never learned the results of the strike photos.

Amazingly, the same intensity and accuracy of tracking flak, which had followed us from the primary to our secondary target, also followed us all the way back to the bomb line. I had learned from infantrymen, while on leave in Paris, that they were horrified to watch American bombers flying through flak while so completely exposed, because on the ground they usually found something to hide behind. Our customary exposures to flak were brief enough, and the near misses few enough, that I had never before felt especially exposed. On this mission, however, that feeling was very strong. We were just like targets in a shooting gallery, and those German gunners were extremely good, so our situation seemed hopeless. Even before we reached the secondary target, I had felt trapped in a nightmare of explosions that could only end with the deaths of all of us. No other result seemed logical or possible; it seemed only a matter of time. As we headed west for the bomb line with no relief, those feelings continued unabated, and I believe they were shared by everyone in our flight; some have told me so.

When we finally crossed the bomb line and the explosions ceased, the surprise and relief were indescribable. It was like being reborn, given another life so unexpected that it was almost unbearably sweet and dear, surely a gift from heaven. However, I still had to find our way home, and even that would not be easy. The stress had so numbed my mind it was hardly working at all. Physical work would not have been too difficult, but the mental work of navigation was almost impossible. I had to force myself to do it, just one simple step at a time, and still missed our airfield by about ten miles, something that didn't occur at any other time. Fortunately, there was still enough light to see the field from that distance, so it didn't matter.

Next, however, we had to land. When Bonde tried to let down the wheels, the nose wheel failed to respond. There was a mechanical backup to the hydraulic system, but the nose wheel couldn't even be cranked down, owing to flak damage. With our touchdown speed of more than a hundred miles per hour, landing a B-26 without a nose wheel was tricky because so much momentum had to be dissipated. But Bonde did it flawlessly. In a normal landing, the initial touchdown was on the main wheels, after which the nose wheel was touched down, then the brakes were applied. Without the nose wheel, we landed as usual on the main gear, but the brakes couldn't be used because this would have forced the nose into the runway and thrown the plane into a high-speed somersault. Instead, after touchdown Bonde held the nose as high as possible without scraping the tail, to obtain maximum braking from air resistance. When the plane had slowed enough to lower the nose without tumbling, he let it down. This gave very effective braking, as some of the nose was chewed off while it scraped and screeched down the runway. Finally, with only a little speed remaining, he applied left brakes to turn off the runway to the left, thus clearing the runway and bringing us to a stop on the grass. Sparks had streamed off the runway as our plane's nose scraped over it, and in the presence of 100-octane aviation gasoline these sparks created a fire hazard. So we all climbed out as quickly as possible.

After jumping to the ground, I looked back as the plane piloted by Joe Grow was coming in. Joe had been flying on our right wing, which he remembers clearly, because he says much of the time he slid above us, using our plane as a shield from the flak, something I have never heard of in any other case. Before landing, he was concerned about the landing gear because he knew his plane had taken a lot of damage. He thus cautioned his flight engineer to be especially sure the landing gear were not only down but locked. Only about fifty feet off the runway his engineer suddenly said over the intercom, "They're not locked!" At that point he wasn't about to go around, so he came on in. By this time, it was dark enough that we were all using landing lights. As I watched, he had barely touched down when the left landing light suddenly dropped. I must have known instinctively what would happen next, because I yelled for us to run, and we all started running away from the runway. Of course, Joe's left landing light had dropped because the left main gear had collapsed. Some of his left wing probably broke off when it struck the runway, and more was chewed off by abrasion. The resulting drag pivoted his plane to the left, which sheared off both the nose wheel and the right main gear. This put the plane on its belly and heading off the runway, toward us.

Since all of this occurred soon after touchdown, the plane still had a lot of speed. A fire engine was parked on our side of the runway, and Joe's plane headed straight for it. Apparently the driver saw it coming and already had his engine running, because he drove away as fast as possible. Some firemen had been standing by the fire truck, and they also started running. So it was quite a sight! The fire truck and firemen were being chased by the plane, while its landing lights brightly illuminated the entire scene. Fortunately, the firemen won that race, probably not by outrunning the plane but mainly by getting out of its path.

Not only was Joe's landing gear damaged, but his bomb bay doors were so damaged by flak before reaching our secondary target that they could not be opened. He says he tried everything he could think of to get them open but nothing worked, so both of his 2,000-pound bombs were still aboard when he landed. This was not a good idea, especially with a belly landing, but there was no choice. The great danger was a bomb shaking loose from the bomb rack, thus becoming armed and exploding. This danger was greatest with our heaviest bombs, because of the strong chance a bomb would break loose and the large explosion that would result. Since Joe's crew and many of us nearby were at considerable risk, it was fortunate indeed that neither of his bombs exploded.

The next morning I went out to examine the planes and found another interesting fact. The skid marks of Joe's plane passed so close to the right of our plane that a crash was probably prevented only by some of Joe's left wing having remained behind on the runway.

After debriefing I always accepted the whiskey offered, usually without much enthusiasm. Following this mission, however, it seemed woefully inadequate, so that evening many of us broke out our own supplies. I felt it might restore a more normal frame of mind, and indeed it proved very helpful. In the early evening my mind was filled with images of the things that had happened and also many things that so easily could have happened—such as being blown apart by a flak shell, which happened that day to Kenneth Fagan, a bombardier friend of mine in Paul Young's plane when it took that direct hit in the nose. His home in Frederick, Maryland, was only about forty miles from mine in northern Virginia, so that flak shell had struck close to home in more ways than one. Fortunately I still didn't know about Fagan's death. Even so, we had seen and done too much for one day. Little wonder that many of us relived the day far into the night, while becoming thoroughly inebriated. The next morning, although queasy, I felt restored and ready for whatever was to come next, but I would never again be quite the same person. This mission had become an important part of my life, having tested and tempered me in fires that cannot be recommended but that can have their own value nonetheless. Death had been so close for so long that it became familiar and has never since been feared in the same way. And all other fears became so trivial by comparison.

In the years since, I have often reflected upon this mission and tried to see it in clear perspective. The time from our primary target to the bomb line was *forty-five minutes,* which I noted and recorded, and the flak remained about equally intense and accurate that entire time. Shortly after the mission, I estimated that during those forty-five minutes the longest interval between near misses was about twenty seconds, and others in our flight agreed with this estimate. Even taking a more conservative view that the *average* interval between near misses was twenty seconds, this would mean a total of about *135 near misses.* This is the best estimate I can give, and I believe it is reasonably accurate. However, I will also agree with anyone who considers it unbelievable, because it is, especially when I add that *no plane was shot down from our flight of seven, and no one was killed or even wounded among the forty-three crewmen in our flight.* In view of the conditions, I can only consider our escape unscathed as a miracle beyond understanding.

By comparison, twenty crewmen were listed missing in action from the planes piloted by Hanisch, McPherson, and Huskey. In the circumstances observed, they must all have been killed, with the exception of the parachutist I saw. In addition, two other crewmen were killed (in Paul Young's plane), and six others were wounded. This contrast between twenty-seven casualties in the other twenty planes, but none in our flight of seven, is even more striking when one considers the conditions. Although we all experienced heavy flak at the primary target, the other three flights met little or no flak while returning to the bomb line, whereas forty-five minutes of intense and accurate flak was concentrated upon our flight. Apparently our encounter with the huge formation of mobile 88s occurred because our entire flight path from primary target to the bomb line was considerably farther south than the return paths of the other flights. Under these conditions, our flight should have had even heavier casualties than the others, yet we had none.

In reckoning plane damage, three were lost at the target and four others were destroyed by flak damage resulting in crash landings in friendly territory. One of these was Paul Young's, another was Clarence Martin's, and the other two were Joe Grow's and our own. Thus, of twenty-seven planes on the mission, seven were destroyed and fourteen others were reported flak-damaged, leaving only six with no damage or minor damage that was not recorded.

Wegenek's role as our lead bombardier requires special mention. I came to believe that the requirements for a great bombardier were harder to meet than those for an exceptional pilot or navigator. During the bomb run a bombardier was under heavy pressure because the success of his flight's mission depended critically upon his performance during those few minutes, for which every life in the flight was being risked. He also knew his bomb run was the most dangerous part of the mission. I'm sure no bombardier thought of these things during a bomb run, but they were there in the background as part of his state of mind. While under this kind of pressure, use of the Norden bomb-sight required delicate eye-hand coordination and often last-minute adjustments requiring good judgment. Many bombardiers could perform well in training on the bombing range, but few could do as well in combat. That ability could not be taught but seemed to depend upon a special type of personality that is inborn and very rare, something like that needed by a relief pitcher in the final game of a World Series. Wegenek had this quality to a greater degree than any other bombardier I knew. Thus he became the best bombardier in our squadron and probably the best in our bomb group. Although the conditions of this mission provided the ultimate challenge to his abilities, he still performed as coolly as if on the bombing range. And his results were perfection, like Robin Hood splitting the arrow. But this was not legend; this was fact. I wish he could read this, but he died in 1981, and I never saw him after the war. Anyway, I'm sure confidence was a great part of his success, so he must have known his abilities better than anyone, without needing to be told.

Bonde stresses something else especially important from a pilot's point of view, having often wondered how the pilots of the six planes following us were able to perform all of that evasive action over such a long time. Bonde himself was being told when to turn, and in what direction, by either myself or Wegenek. In addition to the strain of flying in close formation, all the other pilots had to be constantly alert for a sharp, evasive turn. They had no warning of exactly when it would occur, or in what direction. So they had to be ready for it at any moment, and when the lead plane turned, they all had to react instantly to avoid a crash. The concentration required to do this for even a few minutes was considerable. But we must have averaged more than three evasive turns per minute for forty-five minutes, a total of at least 135 sharp changes of course while flying in close formation. Even if the pilots and copilots took turns in the following planes, it is amazing that they all maintained the necessary concentration for such a long time. They must have been exhausted, both physically and mentally, long before we reached the bomb line, and Joe Grow confirms this.

Within the history of the 391st Bomb Group, and of World War II, this mission appears of interest in at least three ways. First, among the 294 missions flown by our bomb group, the losses on this mission were the heaviest ever sustained from flak alone, and were second only to the Ahrweiler mission of December 23, 1944, when our group was attacked by fighters during the Battle of the Bulge.

Second, it seems possible and even likely that our flight experienced the longest ordeal of intense flak encountered by any group of planes during World War II. I have heard of nothing remotely like it among the other 293 missions flown by our bomb group, or from other sources. In addition, and most convincing to me, is the difficulty of imagining that the conditions causing this ordeal occurred at any other time. In one respect, this mission seems analogous to our group's encounter with many of the remaining German fighters during the Battle of the Bulge. In this case, we must have met a great number of the mobile 88s remaining on the western front, dispersed over an exceptionally large area.

Third, this must have been one of the few times in World War II when bombers, other than dive-bombers, shot back (so to speak) at the very flak guns firing at them. Not only that, but we did it successfully, and from an altitude of about twelve thousand feet. When the four 88s fired at us, we immediately fired back with our bombs, which destroyed the guns and their crews, and our turn toward home evaded their flak shells. Indeed, it is difficult to imagine a more unusual or dramatic result.

Many of my war stories have had sequels, but this one has had two.

Why not? Everything else about this mission was outsized. Not long after the war, I realized I was especially startled and upset by any kind of loud, explosive sound, even something like a dog barking. I couldn't remember being that way before, and when Ginnie mentioned it might have resulted from the war, I brushed it off, like so many of her sensible suggestions. As in most other cases, however, I finally realized she was probably right. So I have come to think of it as a kind of disability, thankfully a very benign one, that has persisted to this day. During the war there were lots of jokes about being "flak happy," and in a mild but real way I suppose I am. After all, it is hardly surprising if that ordeal by flak left emotion-laden engrams somewhere in my brain. Apparently those memories are still aroused, with the emotion still attached, by any kind of loud sound.

The other sequel concerned one of the biggest puzzles about this mission—namely, where all those German guns came from and why they were so concentrated over that particular large area of western Germany during a brief period including February 24, 1945. After fifty years I had become resigned that this question would never be answered, at least not for me. Then, while Ginnie was browsing through a library, she spotted a book titled *The Other Battle of the Bulge*. She knew I had been involved with the well-known one and thought this might interest me, so she brought the book home.

It was written long after the war, in 1986, by Charles Whiting, a military historian. The well-known Battle of the Bulge in the Belgian Ardennes has been highly celebrated in American military history. Although there was a second such battle, Whiting points out that "...the history of that second Battle of the Bulge in the winter of 1944/45 has never [before] been recorded, in spite of the fact that it lasted a month longer than the original Battle of the Bulge and cost the Americans some 16,000 casualties." About twice that number of French soldiers were also lost while serving under American command. Whiting also says, "Yet, strategically and politically, it was a much more significant battle than the original Battle of the Bulge." The situation was so serious that Eisenhower was forced "...to order the first and only retreat of an American army in the whole course of the campaign in Western Europe." And General Patton stated, four days after the battle began, "We can still lose this war."

This "Other Battle of the Bulge" was code-named by Hitler himself as Operation NORTHWIND, a major assault on the U.S. Seventh Army in Alsace-Lorraine, not far south of the Ardennes. This region includes Strasbourg, and the whole area is highly significant to the French, both emotionally and politically, having changed hands between France and Germany a number of times. Hence, this area was delicate to the cause of the Allied military alliance.

The area also includes Colmar, which was stubbornly defended by German forces strongly resisting being pushed back across the Rhine. So this became known as the Colmar Pocket, which to my knowledge was the only name the Allies used for the entire battle taking place around that area. I knew it by that name at the time and thought of it as a difficult but not especially significant action. It would appear now that the name itself probably trivialized this battle and contributed to its remaining obscure for so long. What's in a name? Sometimes almost everything. But there were probably other reasons why this battle became so little known to the American public. When the area ceased being just a "pocket" and became the focus of a major counterattack, initial defensive actions by both American and French troops left a great deal to be desired. By January 25, 1945, the military police had apprehended about forty thousand deserters, which must have been quite embarrassing. So Americans and French alike may have played down the importance of this action, and reports of what actually occurred may even have been suppressed.

In any event, this second counterattack began at 11:00 P.M. on December 31, 1944, while the original Battle of the Bulge was still in progress, though by that time its eventual outcome was no longer in doubt. After a long period of initial disappointment, Allied forces finally stopped and threw back this second attack. Whiting gives no date for completion of the action, but it appears the Germans were finally cleared from Neuf-Brisach, the last town they occupied west of the Rhine, on February 6, 1945, or soon thereafter. Many German armored divisions had been involved in this battle, of which the remainder must have finally retreated across the Rhine. Following such a prolonged period of intense combat, which had thoroughly exhausted both German and Allied troops, it seems safe to assume that German troops were allowed a period of recuperation before moving to new positions. If the armored divisions finally moved north with their mobile 88s, the timing seems reasonable for us to have encountered them there on February 24. I will probably never know whether this is the correct explanation, but it is the only logical possibility that has presented itself in all this time.

Like the "Other Battle of the Bulge," of which it was probably an aftermath, the mission described in this account has taken a long time to appear in writing. Even in Colonel Walker's history of the 391st Bomb Group, only statistical information about this mission is available. Thus our flight's experience has remained almost unknown, except to the few men still alive who were in our seven planes.

Chapter 18
Heading for the Finish Line

By mid-March 1945 the beginning of the war's end in Europe was finally in sight. Both of the major German counterattacks had been thrown back, and the Rhine had been crossed in force. The breakthrough occurred at Remagen, where Americans reached the Ludendorff rail bridge on March 7, 1945, before it could be entirely blown by the Germans. Thus, it was saved long enough to develop the first Allied bridgehead east of the Rhine. Although German damage had made the bridge unsafe for heavy equipment, American engineers quickly built two pontoon bridges, which permitted a massive crossing of the Rhine. Ten days later the Germans destroyed the original bridge by shelling, but by then the damage to their cause was irreparable.

Though these favorable developments were critical, much more fighting remained. In fact, being no longer hampered by winter weather, the pace quickened both in the air and on the ground, and I flew fourteen missions in March, many more than in any other month.

By this time most of us had evolved from peaceful citizens to air warriors, and combat had become our lives. Flying missions was not only our work, it also had become a welcome break from the monotony between missions, and I clearly remember preferring to go on missions instead of staying behind. This was partly because I wanted to finish my tour of missions and go home as soon as possible. But there was also the excitement, sometimes in extremes that started the adrenaline flowing, much like mountain climbing or any other dangerous sport undertaken for recreation.

Occasionally, however, there were more conventional diversions. Apparently the 391st was not a large enough group to merit visits from the famous actors and musicians who traveled the military theaters entertaining servicemen. However, in mid-February our air base was visited by an enjoyable French variety show, the only show of any kind that I saw at Roye/Ami. The act I remember best was the juggler's, because he had a great finale. He was juggling a bunch of balls, and a dog was sitting at his feet, watching intently. At the end, as he was catching the balls and keeping them, the dog jumped up to catch the last ball, and he caught the dog.

Soon thereafter, in early March, I received my third and last three-day pass to Paris, where I was billeted in a fine hotel near the Champs Élysées. This turned out so well that I hardly left the hotel except for meals at a nearby club. As described in a letter home, there was a beautiful ballroom, a good orchestra, and dancing every night. There also were American nurses, Women's Army Corps (WAC) officers, and USO camp show actresses who were staying there, plus local French girls who dropped in. I met one nurse who was a Quaker girl from Philadelphia, and we were so surprised we stopped dancing and just stared at each other. I also met a French girl who had spent several years in England and spoke perfect English. This was a treat because it was the first time I had been able to really converse with a French girl. So we talked most of the evening, after which I walked her home.

In February I had flown my first eight missions as a lead navigator. In an early three of these, I navigated for the element of window planes, while the next five missions were in the lead plane of a flight. Beginning in March, my responsibilities changed again. In the lead plane of each box, one navigator performed conventional navigation while the other did GEE navigation and also GEE bomb-aiming if required. My first ten missions in March were as GEE navigator, mostly for the entire formation but sometimes in the lead plane of the second box. Some missions in this new role were with the highest-ranking pilots in our bomb group. Three were with Major Joe Earll, our squadron commander, and the last one was with Colonel Gerald Williams, commander of the 391st Bomb Group.

Soon after flying with Colonel Williams, I began receiving assignments as the conventional lead navigator for either the first or second box. In this role I made all final navigational decisions, using both my own work and that of the GEE operator. Meanwhile, Bonde and Wegenek also had been carrying greater responsibilities, and on March 31 the three of us flew together as lead crew of the entire formation to bomb troop concentrations near Wurzburg. To be assigned the mission lead was the ultimate seal of approval for any crew, so it was a satisfying climax to our work together.

In April I flew my last five missions of the war, all either deep into Germany or across Germany into Austria. The first of these was on April 7, flying as GEE navigator for the mission leader, Lincoln Mackay, the pilot who had saved me from sliding off that rockface in Greenland. Our target was a railroad marshalling yard at Göttingen, Germany, which we bombed by flights with a mixture of superior and excellent results. Ten planes were damaged by flak and one crewman was wounded.

April 7 was my twenty-third birthday, and it is always surprising to be reminded how much responsibility we were given while still so young. This mission was my eighth as either the conventional or the GEE navigator for complete formations comprised of about 36 planes and 224 aircrew. And lead pilots, of course, carried even greater responsibility. However, some of the things required of us couldn't have been done at all, or as well, if we hadn't been so young. So the powers-that-be may have winced at giving us all that responsibility, but they probably had no choice.

The mission of April 7 was also my last in the B-26. By the end of the war, the eight B-26 groups of the Ninth Air Force contained over 1,000 planes and had dropped a total of 169,382 tons of bombs, while compiling the most accurate bombing record of World War II, with losses to enemy action of only 0.7 percent—the lowest for any combat plane in World War II. During these operations, the 391st Bombardment Group flew 294 missions and received numerous commendations for especially successful missions, overall bombing accuracy, and low accident rate, in addition to a Distinguished Unit Citation for its notable successes during the Battle of the Bulge. Thus, our bomb group served a gratifying role during B-26 operations in Europe that were large in magnitude, highly effective, and conducted—with minimal losses—against tactical targets that were critically important to the success of Allied ground forces.

Beginning a few months earlier, the 391st Bomb Group had begun converting from B-26s to A-26s, the Douglas Invader. An important reason for introducing this plane in Europe, so late in the war, was probably to have A-26 crews combat-trained and ready to transfer to the Pacific when the war ended in Europe. Though we used it briefly in Europe as a medium altitude bomber, the "A" designation meant it was designed primarily as a low-level "attack" plane. It carried only one pilot instead of two, and the pilot could toggle the bombs from the cockpit. It also carried only a single gunner operating four machine guns, two above and two below the plane. In all non-lead planes, the crew was thus reduced from six to two. Lead planes still carried both a bombardier in the nose and a navigator, who sat to the pilot's right, so lead crews were reduced from seven or eight to four. In this way, the same kinds of missions were conducted while endangering many fewer men.

The A-26 was comparable to the B-26 in bombload, horsepower, and landing speeds during both approach and touchdown. But the maximum speed of the A-26 in straight and level flight was 355 miles per hour—about 45 miles per hour faster than the B-26. The range of the A-26 was also greater by 250 miles, which would have been especially important in the Pacific. And the operational weight of the A-26 was 6,200 pounds less. While this lower weight must have contributed strongly to the additional speed, thus improving protection from fighter planes, it may have made the A-26 less rugged than the B-26 and thus more vulnerable to battle damage. In brief, the formal specifications of the A-26 were all similar to or better than those of the B-26. However, the B-26 had proven exceptional in withstanding battle damage, and the A-26 may not have compared favorably in that respect. Thankfully, the point is moot because World War II ended before the A-26's ruggedness was tested under conditions comparable to those encountered by the B-26.

Converting to A-26s took considerable time and effort, partly because it required much shifting of crew assignments. For example, Chapin and Bob Graves remained together, with George Czerniak serving as lead bombardier, while Don Fry acquired his own plane, with Fawcett as his gunner. So one B-26 supplied the crews for two A-26s, with a gunner left over. In addition, it took time for aircrews to become thoroughly familiar with the new plane and its equipment. Yet all this was somehow fitted in while we continued operating at an intense pace in B-26s.

The group was fully converted by April 10, when two missions were flown with the new plane. I missed the first but was on the afternoon mission with Captain Crumal's crew, leading the second box to bomb an ordnance depot at Naumberg, Germany. Unfortunately, the official results of that mission were somehow lost. Thereafter, we made no further use of the B-26, which we missed, having developed a strong loyalty and fondness for it. But the group's effectiveness seemed unaltered by this change, which was made smoothly, and the A-26 proved to be another great plane. None of us gained much combat experience with it, however—only four missions in my case—because the war in Europe was to end soon.

My long-awaited seven-day rest leave on the French Riviera began on April 12. Like everything else in those days, there were separate facilities for officers and enlisted men, with officers going to Cannes and enlisted men to Nice, about twenty miles farther east. The rules called for a first rest leave after twenty-five missions and another one after forty. But the rules weren't being followed, probably because tactical bombing was so critical in the ETO and navigators were in especially short supply. As a result, I had flown forty-one missions and become eligible for two rest leaves before I finally got the first one.

I don't remember the trip to Cannes, but it must have been by air, because on April 11 I was on a long mission to bomb the marshalling yards at Zwickau, Germany, and by late afternoon of the twelfth I was on rest leave in Cannes. There were three fine hotels—the Carlton, the Miramar, and the Martinez—which were adjacent to each other and right on the beach. All were being used for officers on rest leaves, and I was in the Martinez, which had a large, open-air terrace overlooking the Mediterranean, by far the bluest and most beautiful sea I have ever seen.

I was sitting there that first afternoon when an excited buzz of conversation broke out among the tables and I learned that President Roosevelt had died earlier that day. Out of respect for Roosevelt, the French government had announced an immediate countrywide three-day ban on music and dancing. These entertainments had been much anticipated, so this ban at the beginning of my long-overdue rest leave was very disappointing.

That evening some of us roamed Cannes in search of anything interesting that might be open. Finally coming upon a small bar-cafe, we went in for something to eat and drink. The atmosphere proved cold and commercial, hence not at all satisfying, and I was probably in a bad mood at having to settle for something like this. So when I was presented with an outrageously large bill, it seemed like the last straw. I was holding a wineglass, and in my frustration must have started squeezing it. Suddenly it shattered and cut my hand rather badly. When the proprietress saw what had happened, she literally turned white. I guess she knew that servicemen sometimes cleaned out bars and thought this was about to happen. In any event, she hastened to be solicitous and bandage my hand. The experience was almost worth it, just to see her expression when the wineglass shattered and my blood started flowing.

When the three-day ban expired, our hotel resumed music and dancing every afternoon on its terrace facing the sea. That was how I met Nicole, a refined young lady who had come with a girlfriend. I noticed them sitting together and found Nicole especially attractive, so I finally mustered the nerve to ask if I might join them. My French was almost nonexistent, but they were well educated and spoke English, so the talk flowed easily and we quickly became acquainted. After dancing on the terrace, I invited Nicole to dinner at the hotel and then walked her home. We had enjoyed the evening, so we spent most of our time together during the last few days of my leave. My second rest leave was only a month later, and we also spent much of that together.

Because of our different religions and cultures, I'm sure we both knew there couldn't be anything serious between us. But it was an idyll and a welcome change from my life at war, and it couldn't have been spent in a more beautiful place. The sea, coast, and surrounding country were unsurpassed, so we bicycled throughout the area and swam in that lovely sea. It was epitomized by an incident one day while riding our bicycles to Eden Roc, an extraordinarily beautiful spot on the coast. We were holding hands while riding side by side, and as we passed through a small town, an American nurse said in a teasing voice, "You're flying pretty low, Lieutenant." She was right except for one very important thing: The dangers were all far away. I can hardly imagine a better antidote to war than the innocent pleasures of my time with Nicole. Our romantic friendship was an important part of my war, and I include it here for that reason, hoping that if she ever reads this she will still cherish those memories as I do.

On April 16, while I was in Cannes, the 391st Bomb Group moved forward again. The Allied ground troops were moving so fast that our missions from Roye/Ami were becoming unduly long. Thus our group moved forward once more, to an air base near the eastern border of Belgium. Previously used as a fighter base, from which the fighters had moved even farther forward, its location was given as Asch. There was an even closer village—Zwartberg—and the nearest town of any size was Hasselt, about seven miles to the west. Although somewhat primitive, the airfield was adequate for A-26s. Being lighter than B-26s, these new planes did not need runways either as strong or as long as those required by B-26s.

At this new air base the best part for me was the quarters, which were comfortable and even charming. The airfield was next to a planted forest of young pines, and my quarters were in this forest. A pleasant four-man barracks, much like a resort cabin in the woods, it was even conveniently close to our squadron headquarters. My bunkmates were a pilot, Captain "Chuck" Allen, and two bombardiers, Leroy Gresham and "Spinner" Darnall. Though I hadn't known any of these men well before, it proved to be another congenial group. In my April 23 letter, I described our quarters as follows. "We have more room than we ever had before—this setup is really perfect. There are two big hinged windows on the south side of the building, a stove, a walled-off section for baggage, and electric lights. Then in the line of furniture we have a tall shelved clothes locker apiece plus a big writing desk, a big radio, a table and four good chairs." In addition, I had acquired four bedsheets from a fellow going home, so my bed was complete. Indeed, my quarters at Asch were heavenly, especially by our standards at that time. Almost everyone else at Asch, including officers of higher rank, lived much less comfortably in tents. I have no idea how living quarters were assigned, but the four of us appreciated and made good use of ours, which became something of a social center. We had frequent visitors, including Bonde and Wegenek, and our gatherings for talk and card games were sometimes enlivened by shared food packages from home.

While at Asch, promotions also came through for some of us who had joined the 391st at about the same time. Bonde had already become a captain, and now Wegenek received a well-deserved promotion to captain, while I became a first lieutenant. So we all started sporting new hardware on our uniforms.

Though Roye/Ami had offered almost nothing in the way of local entertainment, our location at Asch was much better. Most of us had bicycles and spent much of our spare time visiting nearby areas with companions from the air base. Spring was already in the air when we arrived, and the countryside was beautiful. Also, both Zwartberg and Asch were nearby and offered welcome amenities. In Zwartberg there was a lovely country-style hotel, and one of the villages had a bakery that sold delicious round loaves of bread. I soon learned the right time to get them fresh from the oven, when they were heavenly, so we often tore the bread apart with our hands and ate most of it before getting back to the base.

At the hotel in Zwartberg, I also became acquainted with a delightful couple, Monsieur and Madame Hanot, who were then in late middle age. One Sunday, they invited Gresham and myself for dinner while they were being visited by a niece, Marcella Bodart, and a friend of hers. Monsieur Hanot was winding up a successful career as a mining engineer, and Marcella and her friend were both schoolteachers, so they were well educated and spoke good English. Conversation flowed easily, and Gresham and I found we could even joke with them without fear of being misunderstood. The meal was marvelous, and afterward we spent most of the afternoon in their beautiful garden. That evening they offered us the ultimate luxury for those times. Somehow they had managed to hire a chaffeur-driven Buick to take us into Hasselt to a dance, where we had a fine time with Marcella and her friend. The only problem came at the very end, when we had to ride our bikes six miles from their home to our air base at 2:00 A.M. My letter home says this was "...through a driving mist with no lights, but we didn't mind." The Hanots were such wonderful people and had shown us such a good time, I doubt if anything could have dampened our spirits.

Chapter 19

Ordeal by Headwind

I flew only two missions from Asch, but the first one was another ordeal—this time by weather. It occurred on April 21, shortly after I returned from Cannes. It was only my third mission in the A-26, and I was delighted to be in that plane with Bonde's crew and Wegenek for the first time. As we flew toward the target, it felt natural and comfortable to be with them, but it was even better in the new plane. With its sleeker appearance, higher speed, and smaller crew, it was indeed a refined version of the B-26. I especially liked the smaller crew, with its much great efficiency and cohesiveness. We were flying as lead crew for the third box. With only one gunner, our full crew was four, whereas in B-26s we would have been eight. It was also a special pleasure to once again have a great view—as we all did—in my case from a metal bench on Bonde's right, where the copilot would have been in a B-26.

Our target was the railroad marshalling yard at Attnang-Puchheim in Austria. By that time the front had moved much deeper into enemy territory, so our missions were much longer. Austria was still in German hands, and we had to cross all of southern Germany to reach our target, which we bombed by flights. Looking back to his left, Bonde watched as our 1000-pound bombs caught the tail end of a train as it was leaving the marshalling yard. The train must have been loaded with munitions, because Bonde says "It exploded, one car at a time, from the tail forward, like a string of firecrackers."

Because of the unusually deep mission, our ETA back to base showed we didn't have enough fuel, so we landed at an advance American fighter base near the bomb line. Bonde went to see about refueling and was told there was very little fuel and no overnight accommodations. More important, the base commander had been warned that his airfield would soon be strafed. This was credible because I had recently landed at an advance fighter base just after strafing had destroyed an entire line of C-47 cargo planes. So we were ordered to take off for St. Dizier, much farther west. Our gunners stood on the wings and poured fuel into our tanks from five-gallon cans, each plane receiving very little.

The second flight of our box, led by Jerry Lantz, was still with us. Surprisingly, Jerry had a bombardier-navigator, Gilbert Kinney, but no separate lead navigator. We were so far from our expected route home that I didn't have a map covering the flight to St. Dizier. Kinney had the necessary map and was naturally anxious to keep it. But Bonde insisted and finally directly ordered that it be turned over to me. Of course, this map was essential in determining the compass course that took us all to St. Dizier. So those few ounces of map weighed as heavily in the outcome as anything we carried.

Using the local wind direction and strength, which Bonde had obtained from the weather office at the fighter base, I first computed an ETA for St. Dizier. With our expected flying time, we didn't have nearly the safety factor in fuel normally required on all flights. I told Bonde about this, but he said we had no choice, having been ordered by the base commander to leave.

Meanwhile, the weather had been worsening, and by this time the overcast was so low we didn't dare lose visual contact with the ground. After entering the overcast it would have been extremely dangerous to let down again, because we probably would have hit the ground before having time to see it and level off. The only solution was to keep visual contact with the ground by flying at tree-top level all the way, which made navigation extremely difficult. I couldn't navigate by GEE because of being too low to pick up signals from the ground stations. Likewise, little could be done by pilotage because we were too low to see enough features to match up with our maps. As for dead reckoning, I was unable to determine the actual wind direction and speed under those conditions. So I could only use the wind we had been given to determine our compass course; then we had to fly that course and wait. However, the wind we had been given was almost certainly out of date, because we were encountering a storm front, where weather conditions change rapidly.

Early in this flight, Bonde took the only other precautions available. Having taught B-25 pilots how to obtain maximum fuel economy during long flights over the Pacific Ocean, he was well qualified in that subject. In our plane he reduced the revolutions per minute (rpms) of the engines to slow our airspeed to a minimum, consistent with safety from stalling. This forced all the other planes to follow suit to stay in formation. He also advised the other planes by radio to do everything else they could to save fuel. This included "leaning out the fuel mixture," because a low ratio of fuel to air improved the efficiency of combustion. Also, a steady speed gave better fuel economy than frequent changes of speed. Thus the formation was loosened up to require less jockeying of throttles than when flying in close formation.

Along the entire course to St. Dizier, the only ground feature we could be sure of seeing was a river across our flight path about halfway to our destination. I figured our ETA for that river, but when the ETA came up, the river did not. Every minute counted, but the minutes slipped steadily past until they seemed like forever. I began to wonder if we could have crossed the river without seeing it. That didn't seem possible, but it also seemed impossible that we could be so overdue the ETA. Finally the river flashed beneath us. We were fifteen minutes overdue. That meant thirty minutes overdue at St. Dizier. This would consume all our fuel reserve, so disaster seemed certain.

I began to envision losing every plane in deadstick crash landings, which would be especially dangerous, because our treetop altitude would give little or no chance to choose a favorable landing area. Having nothing else to do, I used our flying time to the river to determine the headwind we must be facing. It turned out we were being slowed by a hurricane-force headwind of seventy-five miles per hour. Needless to say, this was the only time I ever flew in such a strong wind. To have encountered it under these conditions was the worst kind of luck. But there it was! In addition to slowing us down and using badly needed fuel, I feared we would be blown off course, almost a certainty with a wind that strong. And if we missed the airfield at St. Dizier by any significant distance, we would pass right by without seeing it. So even if we could get there, we would probably miss it—double jeopardy. And there were no options. We could only fly and wait for the disaster that seemed inevitable.

Based upon our flying time to the river, I now knew our ground speed, so I had an accurate ETA for St. Dizier. About ten minutes before we were due there, planes started calling to ask for the wind direction in case they had to crash land. That was one thing I could tell them: Make any crash landings right on course. They were desperate because some of their fuel gauges were reading at or near empty, and no wonder. Their situation was worse than ours because our flight had kept a normal tight formation until reaching the fighter base, which must have used considerable fuel from jockeying throttles in the non-lead planes.

Suddenly, just before our ETA, the airfield was straight ahead. I doubt if Bonde even contacted the tower before our flights started landing. All the planes behind us went in as quickly and as close together as possible. Then we landed. The relief was so unexpected and so sudden that it was hard to believe our ordeal was really over. For a time that had stretched interminably, our lives had been held forfeit to time and distance and a hairbreadth on the compass scale. However, fate had intervened on our behalf, and once again our lives would go on.

Jerry Lantz actually ran out of gas while on the approach but managed to reach the runway for a successful deadstick landing. No one could avoid a crash landing more narrowly than that after running out of gas. Also, at least one plane ran out of gas while taxiing. Bonde still has his note that the total flying time, from our air base to our target and back to St. Dizier, was 6¾ hours, by far the longest mission we ever flew.

Perhaps the most astounding fact was that we hit the airfield exactly on course. Bonde likes to say I split the runway, but I can't take credit for that. With an unknown extra wind of such strength, the slightest deviation of its direction from straight ahead would have blown us off course enough to miss seeing the airport. So we were severely jeopardized by its strength, but saved by its being a dead-ahead wind. By the narrowest of margins our fuel and course both held, and once more our entire formation had been saved by something like a miracle.

Though I couldn't know it at the time, I would have to fly only one more mission. And a very good thing, because it seemed impossible my luck could hold much longer.

Chapter 20
From War to Peace

By the end of April the war was winding down, and bombing raids were greatly reduced in number and size. My last mission was flown on April 26, after which our group flew its final one on May 3. The war in Europe ended soon thereafter, with the official signing of an unconditional surrender by Germany, late on May 8, followed by celebration of the Allied victory in Europe, better known as V-E Day, on May 9.

In addition to other major events of that time, President Roosevelt had died on April 12 and Vice President Harry Truman had taken over. Thus ended an important era in American politics. Although Roosevelt had been controversial for many reasons, there seems no doubt he did a fine job of mobilizing and leading our country through the war, so it was fortunate that his death came too late to have any significant effect on the military outcome.

In any event, the war in Europe was now over, and we had to look toward Asia and our war with Japan, the end of which was by no means certain. There was an unavoidable feeling among many of us that we had used up our luck and would be pushing it too hard to go to another war, especially in low-level attack bombers. As so often happens, this feeling was well conveyed by a song that surfaced in our squadron, its origins unknown. Appropriately, it was a parody sung to the tune of *Lili Marlene*, the great German song of World War II that expressed so well the loneliness and longings engendered by war.

The American parody had no title, but it could have been "The Victory in Europe Lament." It went like this:

Please, Mr. Truman, when may we go home?
We have conquered Deutschland
    and we have conquered Rome.
So when will you send another guy?
For we don't like the CBI.
Oh, when may we go home?
When, oh, when, may we go home?

Wishful thinking aside, we fully expected to be involved soon in the war with Japan. Our airfield at Asch offered only prefabricated steel planking between the planes and the earth, which was often muddy after heavy rainfall, so we moved to an airfield with a good concrete runway and an asphalt-surfaced area for parking our planes. This was at Vitry-en-Artois in northern France, near Douai and only twenty miles south of the large town of Lille. Our move was completed on June 5, and a nice result was my billeting there in a three-man room with Bonde and Wegenek.

The move was mainly to obtain a more suitable airfield for training, and during the six weeks I was there we trained intensively in low-level attack operations with the A-26. This consisted mainly of practice in low-level flying and navigation, and we ranged over much of Western Europe just above the treetops. This required pilots to be constantly vigilant, and they probably forgot how to read the altimeter, having no need for it or any time to glance at it. Navigation by pilotage also required exceptional vigilance to catch visual checkpoints, because the field of view was very limited and passed beneath in a blur.

We used floating targets in the North Sea to practice strafing, for which the A-26 was the most formidable plane of its time. Most of the models we used had a solid nose containing six .50-caliber machine guns, with eight others under the wings. In addition, the

---

China-Burma-India Theater of Operations

155

pilot could flip a switch that turned and locked the top turret to fire straight ahead, giving the pilot a total of sixteen forward-firing machine guns, all activated by a single switch. This firepower alone would have been adequate to sink many vessels in the Pacific, where the lesser firepower of B-25s already had proved effective for that purpose.

In one version of the A-26, a 75mm cannon was substituted for machine guns in the nose, which made the A-26 a flying artillery piece. The breech of this gun was to the pilot's right, where it usually served as a seat for the navigator. When the gun was used, the navigator loaded and unloaded while the pilot aimed and fired. We didn't have this version for practice in Europe, but we probably would have used it in the Pacific if the war there had continued much longer. Thus armed, we would even have been able to sink Japanese destroyers or light cruisers. These ships were not protected by armor plate, and they had already proven vulnerable to a 75mm cannon in B-25s.

Though the A-26 could be armed with 5-inch rockets, seven under each wing, we also didn't have those for practice. But of course we had A-26s equipped with a Plexiglas nose and the Norden bombsight, which had been used as lead planes for bombing in Europe and were expected to be used similarly in the Pacific Theater.

In addition to excellent offensive capabilities, the A-26 was superior defensively. With an official maximum speed of 355 miles per hour, about 40 miles per hour faster than the Japanese Zero, it was the fastest American bomber of World War II. It also was heavily armored and so maneuverable it could turn inside an Me-109. Thus, when challenged by fighters, it could outrun them or even dare to dogfight. So the A-26 was by far the most formidable and versatile attack plane or medium bomber of its time.

During our move to Vitry-en-Artois, Colonel Williams attended a conference in Washington, D.C., and announced upon his return that the 391st would be deployed directly to the Pacific. This was expected because it was widely understood that he wanted us into the war with Japan as soon as possible. Aircrews would be sent home by plane or boat, go on thirty-day leave, then fly new planes to an air base somewhere in the Pacific, while ground personnel would go directly to our new air base by ship. Needless to say, there was grumbling about Colonel Williams "maneuvering" us into the Pacific Theater so quickly, and in such dangerous "attack" operations, especially since many of us had nearly completed our tours of missions and would have to begin entirely new tours in the Pacific. This was even interpreted by some as a grandstand play for the colonel to get his first star at our expense. On the other hand, we were combat veterans and already well trained with the A-26. The logic was thus compelling, and though I desperately wanted to live, combat had inured me to undue fear of death and instilled a healthy dose of fatalism. In consequence, I felt ready to do whatever was required, without holding Colonel Williams responsible for the necessities of war. In any event, it seemed advisable to hope for the best but be prepared for the worst.

As it turned out, I was on one of the first planes to return home. With John Collier as pilot, I departed Vitry-en-Artois shortly after July 18, having been overseas for almost a year. This time we used the Southern Ferry Route, with special fuel tanks in the bomb bay to increase our range, because we would fly from Africa to South America without stopping at Ascension Island. In case of an emergency landing, we were also supplied with one-man rafts and enough K rations to last about a week. The trip was made in seven flights, one each day, so no time was wasted.

The first leg of our trip was to Marseille on the southern coast of France. The second leg to Marrakech, Morocco, proved fateful for one plane and crew from our squadron. During the last months of the war, Major Earll had been promoted to lieutenant colonel and had become our squadron commander. Just before V-E Day, he completed his tour of missions and was replaced as squadron commander by Major Manley Richmond. While leading a flight of A-26s over the Mediterranean Sea, Richmond was flying on course at about six thousand feet and only about fifteen minutes from Marseilles when his plane suddenly nosed over and dove straight into the sea. A Mayday was issued and rescue flights arrived soon, but only an oil slick and some landing gear were still floating. The reason for this tragedy will probably never be known, but Richmond was flying our squadron's only A-26 equipped with an autopilot, which may have malfunctioned and been impossible to disengage quickly enough.

Our own flight during that leg of the trip was uneventful but exotic. To reach Marrakech in the northern Sahara, we were over desert for quite some time and in a sandstorm much of the way, although flying at several thousand feet. This was a new experience, and I wondered what the sand would do to our engines, but they tolerated it well.

Because of health regulations for flying into Marrakech, we were instructed to keep the plane closed while taxiing to a hardstand. We were then required to fumigate it with an insecticide to kill any mosquitoes that had stowed away in Marseille. Only after waiting five minutes, to give the insecticide time to do its work, were we supposed to open the plane. The daytime Sahara in the heart of summer is extremely hot under the best of conditions. In addition, the cockpit acted like a greenhouse and soon felt like a furnace. We proceeded to fumigate, and what it was like after that can only be imagined. I have no idea how long we waited to open the cockpit, but it couldn't have been even close to five minutes, after which we would probably have succumbed along with any intrepid mosquitoes unwise enough to join us.

After exiting the plane we stood in the shade of the wing while waiting for a truck to pick us up. We had arrived in about midafternoon, and it was so hot that even in the shade the heat bore in upon us in a way I had never experienced before. Just after being taken to our quarters, there was a light rain; indeed, it was so light that each raindrop disappeared immediately into the parched earth. Even so, it cleared all the sand and dust from the air, as if by magic. Right after this rain, the temperature fell like a stone to a comfortable level. That night it continued to fall, and we slept under several blankets. Thus, the temperature range between day and night must have been about seventy degrees.

On the third day we flew to Dakar, the westernmost point of Africa, in what is now Senegal and was then called French West Africa. This six-hour flight was almost entirely over the Sahara, which looked forbidding but fascinating. One thing I remember well, and have never seen elsewhere, was migrating sand dunes, something I had learned about in a geology course. These are isolated sand dunes in otherwise stony areas, in which the dunes constantly move in the direction of the prevailing wind. From above they have the shape of a flattened U, with the points facing downwind. The incline at the base of the U is not very steep, but the decline on the inner surface is much steeper, because the sand constantly blows up the shallow upwind surface, then falls down the steeper and protected downwind side. Thus the entire sand dune slowly migrates downwind in the direction of the U's points. These dunes were beautiful and sometimes occurred in groups, the individual dunes varying greatly in size. Some of them were also merging together, so there was great variety. I had enjoyed geology, and this aspect of it had unexpectedly come to life before my eyes.

We arrived at Dakar in late afternoon and found it surrounded by jungle that was dark and mysterious, hence fascinating and inviting. Having enjoyed hunting small game as a teenage boy, I had read about expeditions to hunt and collect African animals and had day-dreamed about doing that. After the war I had no further desire for such things, but I would have loved a closer look at the jungle, with its teeming animal life. This, however, was not in the cards. The most disappointing aspect of our trip home was that each day we flew to a new and exotic place but were not allowed to leave the air base because we needed to be rested for the next day's flight. Though understandable, it was frustrating, since it was unlikely we would ever again visit these intriguing places. At Dakar I thus saw the jungle only from a distance but heard many kinds of animal sounds emanating from it at night.

From Dakar we flew the Atlantic the next day (our fourth). With the bomb bay tanks, our cruising range was about nine hours, and depending upon winds our calculated flying time could be from eight to eight-and-a-half hours, so the safety margin was small. The distance was 1,759 nautical miles, and three picket ships were stationed at about 450-mile intervals to assist if someone had to ditch. Fortunately I didn't hear of anyone doing that. Our own flight was uneventful—in fact, boring and very tiring—because each of us had to sit in the same hard seat the entire time. There must have been a great deal of squirming, because no other movement was possible.

For Don Fry, however, the latter part of this trip wasn't boring at all. He was flying a war-weary plane, the oldest A-26 in the 391st. Don test-flew it at Marseille and again at Dakar, to make sure it was all right, and in both cases found no significant problem. However, about thirty minutes from Fortaleza, our destination on the Brazilian coast, the oil pressure of one engine dropped near zero. So Don had to feather the prop and come in on the other engine. The oil pressure of the other engine also dropped alarmingly before he made it to the airfield, which had been cleared for his emergency landing. Both engines were beyond the flying time when they were due to be changed, and no new engines were available locally. Don thus spent two weeks at Fortaleza while waiting for new engines to be obtained from Miami and installed.

After the engines arrived, there were still inexplicable delays. Having been away for so long, and now so close to home, Don was becoming frantic with frustration. Luckily, Colonel Williams came through at that time and Don met him in the shower room, which must have made for considerable informality. Upon inquiring of Don how things were going, the colonel heard his tale of woe and immediately called the operations officer of the air base. Don was nearby when the colonel explained that in the 391st Bomb Group an engine change was done in three hours, and he expected Don to be flying on his wing when he departed the air base at five o'clock the next morning. And that was how it turned out. This was typical of our colonel, who was well known for helping his men in such ways. Paul Young, who came to know him well and greatly admired him, has told me, "I really loved that man. I would have flown through hell with him." Soon after the war, while serving as air attache to Argentina, Colonel Williams was tragically killed with his wife aboard while piloting a DC-3 that crashed into a South American mountainside in bad weather.

My own stay in Fortaleza was only overnight, and my only memory of it was the purchase of a beautiful photograph album from the air base PX. Its cover is a depiction in wood inlay of Sugar Loaf, a famous rock formation just off the Brazilian coast, and it has now contained my World War II photographs for fifty-six years.

On the fifth day, we flew northwest to Georgetown, the capital of British Guiana (now Guyana) on that country's northern coast. This flight was almost entirely over watery jungle, including the complex network of channels comprising the delta of the Amazon River. At that time the whole area was almost uninhabited, and I remember thinking it would be a much worse place for an emergency landing than the Atlantic Ocean. In the ocean, at least there were no trees to hit, and we would be visible to search planes. In the jungle an emergency landing would be disastrous and we would disappear without trace in the heavy foliage. Planes that went down in that area continued to be found for many years after the war, so this concern was well founded.

Our sixth flight was to Puerto Rico, and on the seventh and final day we flew into Hunter Field near Savannah, Georgia. My overseas tour thus became a completed loop, because this had been my point of departure for the Northern Ferry Route, to which I had now returned by the Southern Ferry Route. This air base was much used by returning servicemen, so they were well prepared for us. The first building we entered had a unit (probably a USO) with some of the things we had missed the most. As a farmboy I had drunk mainly milk, but the only drink readily available overseas had been coffee. So without realizing it I had acquired a strong addiction to caffeine that I didn't break entirely until many years later. At Hunter Field there was all the milk we wanted, and it must have been greatly missed because I recall drinking a full quart. They also had ice cream and some other things that most of us hadn't seen for a long time. But the main thing was just being back in our own wonderful country after a long time away, and it felt very, very good.

I was immediately given a thirty-day leave and sent home. One of my greatest pleasures there had been woodworking, which had been a strong interest since early childhood. In fact, I remember trying to make a birdhouse with rough materials and crude hand tools at about age six. Upon reaching fourteen I wanted desperately to make furniture, so my father bought the power tools needed for that purpose. This was still during the Depression, when he could buy all the essential machines from Sears, Roebuck by mail order for only about a hundred dollars. The first thing I made was an ambitious colonial style walnut table, which has long graced the bay window of our living room. Looking at it now, I am astonished that my first project was something so demanding. However, a wonderful thing about youth is that you often don't know something is difficult, so you just do it, like modern children who take to computers as if they were toys.

In any event, I enjoyed woodworking so much that thereafter most of my spare time was spent in the shop until leaving home for college. During that time I made many pieces of walnut furniture and also repaired and refinished antique pieces in our home, such as a grandfather clock made by an ancestor. After starting college I couldn't come home for summers because I was trying to obtain my degree before being caught up by the war. So what with college and the war, I hadn't done any woodworking for about five years and had greatly missed it.

My shop was in the cellar of our old farmhouse, and one day my sister Ruth called down from the head of the stairs, "Ken, what's an anatomic bomb?" My first thought was facetious, that it must take a lot of guts. Then I realized she must mean "an atomic bomb," and it came to mind that just before the war there had been articles in newspapers and magazines about the possibility of releasing the enormous power of atomic energy. During the war I hadn't seen or heard a word on this subject. It thus seemed likely that someone had developed an atomic bomb, and I asked Ruth if that was what she meant. She said she supposed that must be it, because she had just heard on the radio we had dropped something of the kind on Japan. At that point, I realized the war with Japan would be over soon and my life would be spared. Instead of starting a new tour of missions in the Pacific, undertaking low-level attacks against impossible odds, I once again had a future. So I became one of the untold number of Americans whose life was spared by the atomic bomb.

War forces difficult and terrible choices, and the morality of our country's decision to drop its newly developed atomic bombs upon Japan is still debated. That being the case, I feel impelled to note here that when American forces took Okinawa, the last island attacked prior to the planned invasion of Japan itself, General George Marshall reported the Japanese death toll as 100,000 and American losses as 12,500, a ratio of eight to one.

Since Japanese losses resulted largely from refusal to surrender, the ratio could have been even higher during an invasion of the Japanese homeland. It thus seems certain that the atomic bombs saved vastly more Japanese than American lives, as well as saving vastly more Japanese lives than those taken by the atomic bombs themselves.

Though these points are rarely made explicitly, or even mentioned, they seem unavoidably crucial in judging fairly, by hindsight, the decision made while so much blood was being spilled. In truth, having not started that war, America only ended it. And though highly ironic, it would appear this was done as efficiently as possible, thus finally freeing the Japanese people, as well as ourselves, from a war pursued relentlessly by their military leaders.

When the war with Japan ended on August 14, 1945, I was eligible for demobilization, which was done on a point system. Points were earned in a variety of ways, including service overseas and in combat. I had performed sixteen missions as a bombardier and twenty-seven as a lead navigator. For each five missions in lead planes, credit was also given for an additional mission, because of the additional strain and danger of that type of service. So I was credited with another five missions, making a total of forty-eight. This must have translated into many points, because immediately after my thirty-day leave I was mustered out at Fort Meade, Maryland, with an official release date of October 1.

I had always planned to finish college after the war; the only question was where. One reason for choosing the colleges I attended before the war was their low cost. However, after the war I had the GI Bill, which proved an enormous success in every way. As later studies have shown, even our government was repaid many times over by the higher taxes collected from people whose educations had been financed. For me, as for so many others, it was simply wonderful. Under the terms of that bill, I was eligible for support through about five years of schooling, during which tuition, books, and basic living expenses were all covered. Also, throughout my service I had saved almost everything I was paid. Out-of-pocket expenses were almost nothing apart from recreation, and there was little opportunity for that. In consequence I had saved about five thousand dollars, a handsome sum at that time which would nicely supplement the GI Bill. So I could attend any college that would admit me, regardless of its costs.

Having attended a Quaker preparatory school, I was familiar with Swarthmore College, a nonsectarian school founded by Quakers. Located in the outskirts of Philadelphia, it had been favored by many of my prep school classmates, so I visited there as soon as possible and was accepted. Swarthmore opened later than usual that year, on November 1, mainly to accommodate demobilized veterans wishing to enter that fall. What perfect timing for me!

My first days at Swarthmore were unforgettable and an ideal antidote to the stresses of combat. The campus was beautiful, including a large woods with a lovely creek running through it. The teachers and students were intelligent and interesting, and the love of learning was evident everywhere. It was thus a perfect extension of the kind of atmosphere I had come to know and appreciate at George School, which had been left behind five years before. I had two roommates: Joe Bullen had been a Navy pilot, but George Chen had been too young for the war. Both have remained lifelong friends, and Joe still remarks upon the kind of ecstasy I exhibited in those early days at Swarthmore. No wonder, for that was exactly how I felt. All the things I had missed the most for so long were right there, and I couldn't get enough of them.

Much has been written about the readjustment problems of combat veterans, and I have little to add. My war had been relatively clean and comfortable. Of necessity, however, it was often stressful and sometimes extremely violent. And that proved my biggest problem. After being in combat for some time, I truly became "hooked" on it, so much so that when not in combat it became difficult to find satisfaction from normal kinds of recreation. Reading, for example, was simply too dull. Even something like playing poker became less satisfying, compensated only by higher stakes, which were always climbing. When suddenly removed from combat entirely, I felt a real letdown, somewhat like a drug addict's withdrawal symptoms when quitting "cold turkey." In response to this, it is hardly surprising that some men become mercenaries, forever seeking whatever war is available, no matter where it is or whose side they are fighting on. In my case these withdrawal symptoms continued for many months, another similarity with drug addiction. So it was hard to redevelop good study habits, which returned only slowly.

I mention these things not as complaints but simply as interesting observations of a problem that is universal, or nearly so, with returning combat veterans. Its similarities with drug addiction are so striking that I would not be surprised if it results from the release by stress of adrenaline, or some other circulating chemical, that is in itself addictive.

If asked about a treatment for this condition, I would probably suggest girls, because I found them sufficiently exciting to be an ideal way to taper off. After I had enthusiastically dated several during the first few months at Swarthmore, George Chen told me about Virginia

Stern, a girl in one of his classes whom he found especially interesting. This sounded worth following up, so I started paying attention, which was not difficult because we all ate in the same dining room. After meeting a few times by "happening" to sit at the same table, I called her for a date. We had our first one on February 16, 1946 and have now celebrated the fifty-fifth anniversary of that occasion.

There was a small commuter train into downtown Philadelphia, where we went for dinner and a movie. Partway through dinner, I realized this was something very special. We were already so comfortable with each other that she got me talking quite naturally about a lot of things—probably too much. I had just read about the record fecundities of Russian women and the exceptional longevity of people in three isolated mountainous regions of the world, and apparently I regaled her about these. Though she still kids me about the unusual topics for a first date, she also admits to having been fascinated. So we learned quickly that we could enjoy talking about almost anything.

The next morning I called early to ask if we could meet for breakfast. She said she was already up, having taken an early morning walk in Crum Woods. Much later, she explained she had taken the walk because she couldn't sleep and wanted to think about the evening before. She already felt this would be a turning point in her life, as I had felt during our first evening together. So we met for breakfast and never looked back.

Thereafter we met for almost every meal and did most of our studying together, in addition to the usual kinds of dates. What a way to be rehabilitated! Ginnie used to claim, with a twinkle in her eye, that this was all she was trying to do. If word ever got around that rehabilitation could be that much fun, wars would become entirely too popular. It was an ideal, magical sort of time, which ended all too soon when I received my college degree in June 1947. I then started graduate work at the University of Chicago, while Ginnie stayed on to finish her degree at Swarthmore, which in the normal course of things would have taken two more years. By Christmas, however, the separation became too much. So we became engaged and were married in June 1948, after which she completed her degree at the University of Chicago. Thus began our new, and even more deeply satisfying, life together.

Chapter 21
The Bride Price

This story from the war has been left for last because Ginnie needed to be introduced before it could be appreciated.

Our group's move from Roye/Ami to Asch had begun while I was on rest leave in Cannes and was well under way when I returned. Upon arriving at Asch, I noticed two attractive pictures leaning against the base of a tree, near the barracks to which I was assigned. When they were still there several days later, it seemed obvious they had become separated from their owner, probably someone in the fighter group occupying that air base before us. Also, they badly needed protection from the rainy weather, so I hung them in my barracks. One was an original oil painting of a mountain scene, while the other was a well-done reproduction of a pastoral scene in the old Dutch style. Both were quite nice, and I became attached to them. People came in and out of our barracks frequently, so most of the officers in our squadron knew about them quite soon.

About a month later, shortly before we moved to Vitry-en-Artois, I was visited by one of our squadron's administrative officers, who claimed the pictures were his. This seemed strange because I had found the pictures close to our squadron headquarters where he worked, so it was hard to imagine he would not have seen them there.

Also, as I recall he had no explanation of how he obtained them or could have lost them where I had found them.

He didn't actually demand the pictures, but it was clear he wanted me to turn them over. He said he would be returning home soon and had a recreation room where these pictures would be ideal for his purposes. I remember thinking it odd that he seemed to consider having a use for them as a justification for claiming them. Of course, the pictures may have been his earlier, and I may have misinterpreted the situation entirely, but I couldn't help being skeptical. In any case, a quick decision was called for. If I had told him what I thought, or even taken time to think about it, this would have been tantamount to calling him a liar. And this would not have been wise, because administrative officers made decisions that could strongly affect our lives. So I gave him the pictures.

About two months later, I was assigned to fly home in one of the very first planes to leave Vitry-en-Artois. Most flying officers trickled home later by air, and many were sent even later by ship. Though Bonde was then a captain whereas I was a first lieutenant, even Bonde had to wait much longer for transport and finally returned by ship on a long, overcrowded, and uncomfortable voyage. So how did I get such a plum assignment to fly home? I can't know for sure, but I will always believe it was either an outright payoff or a favor for my returning his pictures. If his claim was invalid, he may also have felt embarrassed by my presence and wanted me away as soon as possible.

In any event, by getting home so soon, I was able to start at Swarthmore that fall, thus saving up to a full year in completing my college degree. Much more important, I met Ginnie before either of us had made other attachments or commitments. If I had been delayed as long as Bonde, it seems extremely unlikely this would have happened, and my whole postwar life would have been different. It is painful even to think of not having married Ginnie, but I'm sure that would have been the result if I hadn't relinquished those pictures.

Life works in such strange ways! I got up one morning at Asch, not knowing that during the day I would turn over those pictures to someone else. And I couldn't have imagined that this simple act would be one of the most beneficial single events of my lifetime. However, I firmly believe it was, and I realized later what an enormous debt of gratitude I owe that officer who asked for the pictures. Indeed, it was the greatest bargain I can imagine. The payment that some cultures require an aspiring husband to give for his bride is called the "bride price." So I sometimes tease Ginnie that her bride price was only two pictures.

We were married in Plainfield, New Jersey, in the Quaker meeting house long used by her family, since her mother and father, like my own, came from Quaker backgrounds. We sat together on a bench facing our assembled families and friends. Following a period of silence that lasted many minutes, we stood facing each other with hands joined, and while looking into each other's eyes, spoke the traditional Quaker marriage vow. I said:

In the presence of God, and these our friends,
I take thee, Virginia, to be my wife, promising,
with divine assistance, to be unto thee a loving and
faithful husband as long as we both shall live.

Ginnie then took me for her husband with the reciprocal vow, after which we placed wedding rings on each other's fingers, kissed, and sat down. During a final period of silence, someone in attendance gave a brief inspirational message. The ceremony ended when we shook hands with each other, after which everyone rose and shook hands with others nearby.

Many years later, the story of the bride price continued. Ginnie had an aunt, Mildred B. Miller, a professional artist whose Impressionist-style paintings we love. In 1943 she had set aside her career "for the duration" to do war work as a draftsman. Where? In the engineering department of Glenn L. Martin, of course. After the war she moved to a small fruit ranch near Valley Center, California, not far from San Diego, and we visited her there for three weeks during our summer-long honeymoon in the West. During that time she painted a fine portrait of Ginnie, while I painted the guest bedroom she had recently added to her bungalow to accommodate us. When Aunt Mildred died fourteen years later, Ginnie inherited the paintings still in her possession, including an oil rendition of a B-26 over a burning target. So the story came full circle, and the bride price was returned in kind many times over. Recently we donated many of those paintings to Swarthmore College, where we had met during that wonderful postwar period so infused with purpose and promise.

Epilogue

L ike so many other couples after World War II, Ginnie and I plunged into our lives and careers with optimism and enthusiasm. After completing our educations in Chicago, where we lived in a small room under slumlike conditions, my civilian research position at the Aero-medical Laboratory was most welcome. We moved to a spacious four-room apartment constituting the top floor of an old house in Yellow Springs, Ohio, an easy commute for me and the location of Antioch College, where Ginnie worked. Having studied mathematics and science, she first did statistical work for the college, then became a research assistant at Fels Institute, a private institution near the Antioch campus, where she studied the physiology of stress. It was a pleasant and satisfying life, but after several years we both wanted the more stimulating atmosphere of a university.

I felt the need for further research training, and those postwar years generated unprecedented support for science. My first postdoctoral fellowship, from the National Science Foundation, supported a year at Brown University, followed by three years at the Johns Hopkins School of Medicine, under a fellowship from the U.S. Public Health Service. At Johns Hopkins I was fortunate to work with Stephen Kuffler, a renowned neurophysiologist with whom I acquired the necessary background and skills to conduct research in retinal neurophysiology. Finally, in 1958, we moved to San Francisco. After a long and meandering path, I had found just the right work for me and the ideal place to pursue it, namely the University of California's Medical School in San Francisco (UCSF), where I became a professor engaged primarily in research. This career proved fruitful and enjoyable, and I never again wished for any other.

How we came to settle in San Francisco was a story of its own. We had married early in the summer of 1948, while still in school, and spent our honeymoon touring the West in an old car. This proved a wonderful experience, our expenses being minimized and our pleasure maximized by many beautiful nights under the stars in park campgrounds, which were then delightfully uncrowded. Though we were in San Francisco for only one day, it was "love at first sight," which can be wise, as we had learned. So we decided that of all the cities we knew, this was where we most wanted to live. Nine years later, when I became eligible for a university position, we had not forgotten that. Of course, I investigated faculty openings in my field that had been announced in some way. But I also wrote to Leslie Bennett, chairman of the Physiology Department of UCSF's Medical School, inquiring if they might have openings in the near future. The letter was completely "blind" because I had no personal contact at that school. So the chance of success was almost zero, but I had to give it a try.

Imagine my surprise when he replied that about fifteen months hence they would need someone specializing in neurophysiology. The lead time was perfect, and it seemed too good to be true. However, his letter was distinctly cool, pointing out that they expected many applicants to be attracted by San Francisco, etc. When Ginnie read his letter, bless her loyal heart, she was furious that I should be treated as only another person wanting to live in San Francisco. So she wanted me to write back in high dudgeon and let him know what kind of person he was dealing with. I thought about how to do this in a way that would intrigue him, but with a maximum of diplomacy and a minimum of dudgeon. Finally, I wrote the letter in my lab and read it over the phone to Ginnie, who had calmed down by then and thought it hit just the right note. Apparently it did, because his next letter was entirely different, warm and respectful and setting up a recruiting visit to San Francisco. Later, he visited us in Baltimore and offered me the position about a year before completing my work at Johns Hopkins. At UCSF he became a good friend and staunch supporter, and this relationship continued throughout my career there.

Ginnie and I enjoyed together the satisfactions of my career, and our home also proved a great joy. Since 1960 we have lived only about three blocks from the medical center, so I often walked home for lunch, and it was ideal for the many times I worked in the evenings, sometimes conducting experiments that lasted almost all night. Our house was built shortly before the great earthquake of 1906, and before moving in, we considerably remodeled it. Much of that work was done with my own hands, and I have continued to make improvements ever since. After retirement, I began designing furniture and made many one-of-a-kind pieces for specific places or purposes in our home. Ginnie collaborated in one of these designs, a cradle we jointly patented. Later, I also designed and made stained-glass windows for both our own and a neighbor's home.

Here we raised our two sons. Their marriages have brought us four daughters-in-law whose national origins include Romania, Vietnam, India, and Jordan, and six grandchildren who delight and occasionally exhaust us. So our personal world continues to expand, as seems necessary and increasingly typical of these times.

When I reflect now upon World War II, my mind still floods with feelings. I well remember how the blood ran rich and full, and every moment was cherished, an oft-remarked reaction to death seeming imminent. And I continue to feel intense pride for whatever small role I played in bringing that conflict to a successful conclusion for my country and the free world of that time. But I am also overwhelmed with humility and gratitude, to whatever powers rule our lives, to have survived that war intact. I can never know how it occurred, but it made possible a long life filled with more satisfactions and pure joy than I could have imagined possible. Having been given such a fortunate life, there is little more to be said. As the end inevitably approaches, I look to the past with a deep sense of fulfillment and to the future with great interest in what it yet may hold.

Acknowledgements

I n this, as in so much of my postwar life, my wife, Ginnie, has been a true partner. Acting as my personal editor, she read several drafts and made many helpful suggestions. Giving criticism where needed and encouragement when needed, she assisted immeasurably, for which no thanks could be enough.

Three pilots from the 572d Squadron of the 391st Bombardment Group also made notable contributions. The two with whom I flew most, Kenneth R. Chapin and P. K. Bonde, supplied details of our missions from the pilot's point of view. Lester Stanford, who flew with our squadron from its arrival in England in January 1944 until February 1945, also assisted from his long experience and exceptional memory. And Bob Cox, who worked in the photographic unit of our bomb group, provided details of how photo-reconnaissance was conducted.

James P. Muri, the only surviving pilot of the four B-26s that attacked the Japanese fleet at Midway, filled out details of that notable event in B-26 history. And Richard S. Bailey, a pilot who survived the B-26's troubled early days at Tampa, Florida, provided details of why many of his fellow airmen of that time were not so fortunate.

Scott Thompson, archivist at the Pima Air and Space Museum near Tucson, Arizona, generously provided information and photographs from their Martin B-26 Marauder Archive. And Ray Wagman, archivist at the San Diego Air and Space Museum, supplied many technical and historic details of B-26 operations during World War II.

For "The Ordeal by Flak of Flight 4," I conducted telephone interviews with everyone I could find who had been on that mission. In addition to Chapin and Bonde, this included six other pilots, two copilots and three gunners. These men are Orville J. Cambier, Donald Fry, Jr., Robert E. Graves, Joseph A. Grow, Clyde Kirkbride, Stuart Main, Clarence L. Martin, Naurbon L. Perry, Arlo Sienknecht, Kenneth L. Taplin, and Paul R. Young.

For "Ordeal by Headwind," similar help was provided by Jerry Lantz, who piloted the lead plane of the flight that followed our flight to St. Dizier.

Major General John O. Moench, USAF (retired) and president of the B-26 Marauder Historical Society, gave valuable consultation and advice.

Special thanks are due to Eric Hammel, my editor at Pacifica Military History, who helped with final revision of the manuscript and guided all other aspects of publication.

Glossary and Guide to Abbreviations

A-20 USAAF Douglas Havoc twin-engine attack plane used as a light bomber in Europe during World War II

A-26 USAAF Douglas Invader twin-engine attack plane used as a medium bomber in Europe, beginning in November 1944

B-17 USAAF Boeing Flying Fortress four-engine heavy bomber

B-24 USAAF Consolidated Liberator four-engine heavy bomber

B-25 USAAF North American Mitchell twin-engine medium bomber

B-26 USAAF Martin Marauder twin-engine medium bomber

Bomb line The line between friendly and enemy territory

Box Formation of airplanes consisting of three flights, each containing six planes

C-47 USAAF Douglas Dakota twin-engine cargo/transport

CLARION Aerial operation against Germany by all available Allied aircraft, conducted February 22 and 23, 1945

Clubmobile Vehicle operated by the American Red Cross to supply doughnuts and coffee to front-line troops

CO Commanding officer

CRT Cathode ray tube; the device that supplied the viewing screen for the GEE navigation system

CTD College training detachment, one of which was attended by every aviation cadet

DC-3 U.S. Douglas civilian commercial version of the C-47

Dead reckoning Navigation by using wind speed and direction to calculate the desired compass course of an airplane and its speed over the ground

Deadstick landing Landing made without engine power

Element Formation of three airplanes in which a "wing" plane flies on each side of, and slightly behind, the lead plane

Enigma Coding machine used by German and Japanese forces during World War II

Escape kit Packet of items to assist downed Allied airmen in evading capture and returning to friendly forces

Escape map Silk map, printed on both sides, that was part of the escape kit

ETA Estimated time of arrival

ETO European Theater of Operations

E-6B Hand-held mechanical computer that assisted with computations for dead reckoning

F-5 USAAF photo-reconnaissance variant of the Lockheed P-38 Lightning fighter

Flak helmet Steel helmet used by bomber crewmen

Flight Formation of six planes consisting of two three-plane elements, one behind the other

GEE The first electronic method of aerial navigation, developed in England and used in Europe during the final years of World War II

GI Government issue

GI Bill Federal legislation that gave veterans financial help, most notably with education, after World War II

Hardstand Parking area for an airplane, usually surfaced with concrete or asphalt

Intervalometer Instrument to provide an electrical signal after a preset interval

IP Initial point from which a bomb run was begun

Killing the drift Use of the Norden bombsight to compensate for wind and put the plane on track directly toward the target

Killing the rate Use of the Norden bombsight to determine the plane's speed over the ground, so that bombs could be released at the correct time

Leaning out the fuel mixture Reducing the ratio of fuel to air to improve fuel economy

Marauder Man A member of the aircrew of a B-26 Marauder medium bomber

Mayday Emergency call for assistance

Me-109 German Messerschmitt single-engine fighter plane produced by Bayerische Flugzeugwerke; known in Germany as Bf 109

Milk run Slang term used by Allied airmen to describe an easy mission

MP Military police

Norden bombsight Instrument used in heavy and medium American bombers for precision bombing during World War II

Northern Ferry Route A route used to transfer planes between the United States and Europe, with outbound stops in Georgia, Maine, Labrador, Greenland, Iceland, and Scotland

P-38 USAAF Lockheed Lightning twin-engine fighter

PDI Pilot's directional indicator, used to show the pilot the course corrections required by the bombardier during a bomb run

Picket ship Ship stationed at a fixed location to handle emergencies that might arise along a sea route

Pilotage Aerial navigation by visible landmarks

Pilot's cross A rainbow-like circle around the shadow of a plane upon clouds below

Piper Cub USAAF Piper J-3 or J-5 two-place monoplane used to give all aviation cadets their initial flight instruction

PX Post exchange, a facility on most military bases where personal necessities could be purchased

Resistance The organized resistance in France to the occupying German forces during World War II

rpm Revolutions per minute

Slot position The position, in a flight of six planes, of the plane flying behind and slightly below the flight leader

SOP Standard operating procedure

Sortie A mission performed by a single plane, even when the plane is part of a formation

Southern Ferry Route A route used to transfer planes between the United States and Europe. On the return route, stops were at Marseilles, Morocco, French West Africa (now Senegal), Brazil, British Guiana (now Guyana), Puerto Rico, and Georgia

Strike photos Photographs taken from the lead and slot planes of each flight to record the flight's bombing results

Sweat job Slang term used by B-26 crewmen to describe a stressful event

Taxi sheet A sheet of paper showing the crews assigned to a given mission and the assigned position of each crew's plane in the formation

TBF USN Grumman Avenger single-engine torpedo/light bomber

TLS Time-lapse signal from a pair of ground transmitters that provided the basis for GEE navigation

Toggleier Slang term for a bombardier who only toggled the release of his bombs without participating in bomb aiming

Trim tab Portion of a plane's control surface—for example, a portion of the rudder—which permits the plane to be "trimmed up" for straight-and-level flight

USAAF United States Army Air Forces

USAF United States Air Force

USO United Service Organizations, which provided recreational facilities for servicemen

V-1 German "buzz bomb," an unmanned aircraft employing a jet engine; first used against England on June 13, 1944

V-2 The first true ballistic rocket used in wartime; developed in Germany, it was much used against London beginning September 8, 1944

V-E Day May 9, 1945, when the Allied victory in Europe was celebrated

V-J Day August 14, 1945, when the Allied victory in the Pacific and Asia was celebrated

WAC Women's Army Corps

Window Metallic chaff released by a bombing formation to confuse German gunners using radar-controlled antiaircraft weapons

Wing loading The weight supported per unit area of an airplane's wing

Bibliography

Brown, Virginia W. "Marauders at Midway." In *Marauder Thunder*. Rockville, MD: B-26 Marauder Historical Society, January 1999.

Caidin, Martin. *The Ragged, Rugged Warriors*. New York: E. P. Dutton, 1966.

Caidin, Martin, and Edward Hymoff. *The Mission*. Philadelphia and New York: J.B. Lippincott Company, 1964.

Childers, Thomas. *Wings of Morning*. New York: Addison-Wesley, 1995.

Dinou, John C. "A Quaker at Utah Beach." In *Flight Journal*. Ridgefield, CT: June 2002.

Doolittle, James H. *I Could Never Be So Lucky Again*. New York: Bantam Books, 1991.

Dorr, Robert E. *U.S. Bombers of World War Two*. London: Arms and Armour Press, 1989.

Editors. *B-26 Marauder in Action* (video). Arvada, CO: Boomerang.

Ethell, Jeffrey L. *Jane's World War II Aircraft*. Glasgow: HarperCollins, 1999.

Forsyth, Robert. *Battle Over Bavaria*. East Sussex, England: Classic Publications, 1999.

Francis, Devon. *Flak Bait*. New York: Duell, Sloan and Pearce, 1948.

Freeman, Roger A., with Trevor J. Allen and Bernard Mallon. *B-26 Marauder at War*. New York: Charles Scribner's Sons. Publication date not known.

Fuchida, Mitsuo, and Masatake Okumiya. *Midway: The Battle That Doomed Japan, The Japanese Navy's Story.* Annapolis, MD: Naval Institute Press, 1955.

Hammel, Eric. *Air War Europa: Chronology 1942–1945.* Pacifica, CA: Pacifica Press, 1994.

Havener, J. K. *The Martin B-26 Marauder.* St. Petersburg, FL: Southern Heritage Press, 1998.

Lord, Walter. *Incredible Victory.* Short Hills, NJ: Burford Books, 1967.

Mendenhall, Charles A. *Deadly Duo: The B-25 and B-26 in WW-II.* Osceola, WI: Specialty Press, 1981.

Moench, John O. *Marauder Men: An Account of the Martin B-26 Marauder.* Longwood, FL: Malia Enterprises, 1999.

O'Leary, Michael. "Mission with the Marauder: Airborne with the World's Last Flying Martin B-26 Marauder." In *Air Classics,* January 1998.

Rhodes, Richard. *The Making of the Atomic Bomb.* New York: Simon & Schuster, 1986.

Sakai, Saburo, with Martin Caidin and Fred Saito. *Samurai.* New York: E. P. Dutton and Company, Inc., 1957.

Scutts, Jerry. *B-26 Marauder Units of the Eighth and Ninth Air Forces.* London: Osprey, 1997.

Tannehill, Victor C. *The Martin Marauder B-26.* Arvada, CO: Boomerang, 1997.

Tuleja, Thaddeus. *Climax at Midway.* New York: Berkley, 1961.

Walker, Hugh H., ed. *391st Bombardment Group: History W.W.II.* Austin, TX: 391st Bombardment Group Association, 1974.

Whiting, Charles. *The Other Battle of the Bulge: Operation Northwind.* Chelsea, MI: Scarborough House, 1990.